THEATER OF THE NIGHT
What we do and do not know about
DREAMS

THEATER OF THE NIGHT

What we do and do not know about

DREAMS

S. Carl Hirsch

Illustrated with
reproductions of famous paintings

Rand McNally & Company
Chicago / New York / San Francisco

For Charlotte, Terry, Amy, Lucy, Peter
—beautiful dreamers, all.

Library of Congress Cataloging in Publication Data

Hirsch, S. Carl.
    Theater of the night.
    Includes index.
    SUMMARY: Examines past and present attitudes
toward the phenomenon of dreaming, current dream research,
and myths and legends associated with dreams.
    1. Dreams—Juvenile literature. (1. Dreams)
I. Title.
BF1091.H55   154.6'3   76-28188
ISBN   0-528-82012-5
ISBN   0-528-80012-4   lib. bdg.

Jacket illustration by John Dresser

Contents

Acknowledgments

To many of the men and women doing major scientific work in the field of sleep and dreams, I owe a debt of gratitude. Dr. Allan Rechtschaffen at the University of Chicago offered wise guidance as well as a critical reading of the script. Dr. Rosalind D. Cartwright, University of Illinois, Circle Campus, gave me every possible assistance, including some opportunities for experimental work.

The Michel Jouvet group at the University of Lyon conveyed their enthusiasm and a high sense of unfettered inquiry. I am grateful to the U. S. Navy's Dr. Laverne C. Johnson and his associates at San Diego, Dr.'s Ardie Lubin, Paul Naitoh, Julie Moses. I also want to thank Dr. Peter Hauri at Dartmouth; Dr. Harry Cohen at the University of California, Irvine; Dr. Misha Radulovacki at the University of Illinois Medical School; and Dr. Daniel F. Kripke at the University of California, San Diego for their time and their patient assistance. The staff of Dr. William C. Dement was helpful, and my special thanks to Jeff Jenest. Peter L. Hirsch assisted with translations. Very useful information was offered by the National Institute of Mental Health, the Brain Information Service, UCLA, as well as the many investigators who sent me their scientific papers and their suggestions.

Finally, my deep appreciation to Stina L. Hirsch, who helped in a thousand ways at every stage in the metamorphosis of this book.

Illustrations

In Quest of the Dream

As a large fish moves along the two banks of a river, the right and left, so does that person move along these two states, the state of sleeping and the state of waking.

— The Upanishads

You walk into a darkened theater and take your seat. For some time you sit in drowsy comfort, cradled by the silence and the shadows.

At length the curtain rises. The action begins—and what a play it is! Performers come and go, one of them remarkably like yourself. There is little sense to what is being said, and less to what is being done.

In aimless fashion the story unfolds. The plot is sheer fantasy. The players are soberly busy with a lot of puzzling nonsense that leads nowhere. And yet it all seems real as life. Abruptly the play comes to an end.

You will learn in time that you yourself were the producer, playwright, and director. The scenery, the props, the cast—they were all your own creations. But mysteriously, you understand little of what was going on!

This was a dream. For all its puzzling qualities, this was no rare or extraordinary event. In fact, the most remarkable feature of the dream is that it is the common and usual experience of everyone! We share this nightly occurrence with the people of the entire world, and with those who have lived in every age. All of us are regular patrons of this same theater of the absurd.

The next show? Yes, of course, it will be presented tonight. Admission is free. What's more, you won't even have to leave your warm bed.

A RESTLESS RIDDLE

It is morning—time to face some realities of the day. But you are still mulling the truth about dreams. Clearly, they are *not* simple entertainments, cleverly designed to brighten up the long night. You do not really own a private dream theater that caters to your comfort. The "plays" are not all pleasing. Many are just plain dull; some are dismal. Others fill you with fear. Far from being "command performances" under your control, it is you who are commanded to attend. When they are over, you may be shaken, joyous, anxious, refreshed, unmoved. Mostly, you are mystified.

"I went to bed in order to sleep," you tell yourself. "I switched off my weary body and my brain."

But something went wrong. During the hours of darkness, your brain suddenly became very active. In your mind's eye appeared a vivid set of images. You had intended to sleep like a log—passive, senseless, resting. Instead, you lived through a series of powerful experiences, reacting as though you were wide-awake. Why?

Clearly, the sleeping brain has a mind of its own. The mental processes of sleep are different from those of wake-

At the Concert Européen by Georges-Pierre Seurat, Collection, The Museum of Modern Art, New York, Lillie P. Bliss Collection

Whence are we, and why are we? Of what scene
The actors or spectators?

—Percy Bysshe Shelley, *Adonais*

fulness. Dreams occur in sleep—or at least in a portion of it. And if dreaming seems strange, that is because it is a type of brain activity about which we still know very little.

Our hope for understanding lies in the fact that the dream is an occurrence as natural as eating or breathing. We have been able to study and understand many other natural processes and bodily functions, and it seems possible that dreaming will also lend itself to the same search for knowledge.

"But dreams?" you may ask. "Those vagrant visions of our darkest hours, mocking and wispy, elusive and beguiling. Where will we ever find dream probers who will pursue the truth? Where are the men and women who have the stubbornness and the skill to hunt night's fading images—shadows that can hardly be fixed in the mind, let alone cornered, captured, trapped?"

Luckily, dream stalkers do exist.

CENTERS OF THE QUEST

Sleep and dream research is a ceaseless activity that goes on morning, noon, and all through the night.

It is forenoon as I arrive at the medical school of the University of Lyon in central France. I am escorted through double doors marked *Privé* into a long series of laboratories that branch from a high-ceilinged corridor.

A dozen of us gather around a table for the French version of the mid-morning coffee break. The voices are charged with zeal for the work that has paused for only a moment.

This is probably the most famous of the world's research centers devoted entirely to the study of sleep and dreams. Its distinct quality is quickly apparent. Here, many specialists probe from a great number of directions the dark mysteries surrounding sleep and dreams.

One young scientist comments on the curiously differing sleep patterns in various strains of mice of the same species. An American student talks knowingly about her efforts to discover dreamlike patterns *in utero*—in animals not yet born.

We watch as a physiologist rapidly sketches a cat brain on the chalkboard. He recounts with some amazement what showed up on an electronic monitor attached during the night to that portion of a cat's brain suspected to be the center of dreamlike activity. He feels that he is possibly nearing the end of a long search. And he muses about the irony of "using the brain to seek knowledge about the brain."

A woman associated with this research center waves us a cheery *au revoir*. She hurries off to the hospital across the boulevard where she will check the dream patterns of a number of accident victims who have suffered brain damage.

A young professor comes in for a cup of coffee and talks about his latest work on the biological origins of dreaming in prehuman species. A short man in a white laboratory coat is a chemist leading a research project on changes that occur in certain glandular fluids during periods of dreaming. His remarks, and the responses of the others, reveal how closely related these many workers within the Lyon research center are, as well as their kinship with investigators in laboratories throughout the world. The chemistry discussion recalled to me a talk a few weeks earlier with a scientist in Chicago who is studying the brain fluids of sleeping cats. Chicago and Lyon, San Diego and Moscow, Boston and Kyoto—all are in close touch with one another, scientifically speaking.

As for myself, I have discovered one of the most fascinating of scientific fields. For all the newness of this research, it is highly organized in well-staffed, well-equipped centers. The programs appear to be clearly defined as to goals, and much of the experimentation seems brilliantly planned. A good deal of this work, both in the United States and elsewhere, is funded by governments.

On an unseasonably hot day in January, I am on my way out on a long finger of land between bay and sea. Here, at Point Loma, California, is the Navy's hospital. In the sleep lab, the research team is gathered around a large computer that is spelling out the results of an experiment in sleep loss. Electronic signals from the fatigued bodies and brains of a group of Navy volunteers, kept awake for a series of days and nights, will provide the data.

In a huge Boston hospital, I talk with doctors probing the nightmares of war veterans who repeatedly relive in their dreams the terrors of battle.

In Moscow's skyscraper university, I am guided through laboratories that examine the biochemistry in the sleeping brains of turtles, lizards, and leghorn hens.

There is a place in Brooklyn, New York—the Maimonides

Mental Health Center—which conducts experiments seeking to answer the question: Can one person invade another person's dreams? Throughout the night wakeful senders of thought messages seek to communicate with the sleeping receivers. Do they truly make contact? The results are still unclear.

In the city of Los Angeles, I observe the delicate exploration of nerve pathways controlling sleep and dreams. The lab worker here uses a wire finer than baby's hair to study electrical impulses from a single living cell in the brain of a sleeping squirrel monkey.

This is a small portion of sleep and dream research. The results from all these studies are not often spectacular. And yet they have added significantly to our knowledge. This is, after all, a very new field of scientific study. The work has hardly begun.

THE PUZZLE UNFOLDS

Odd, bewitching, and bothersome, our dreams are an itch of curiosity that needs to be scratched. Perplexing as it is, the puzzle of dreams has been made even more complex by modern research.

In an earlier and simpler world, people believed in two separate states of existence—sleeping and waking. It now appears that dreaming is distinct from both. In dreaming, the body is "asleep," but the mind is "awake."

It was this bewildering combination that first drew me

toward a closer look at today's dream research. I was to learn that many of the scientific investigators speak of dreaming as a "third state" of being. We will soon see what they mean. In our venture into modern sleep-dream research, we will be looking over the shoulders of scientists. We will observe how the dreaming brain is studied and why its functions are so puzzling.

Even more questions are provoked by that strange product of the dreaming brain—the dream itself. What is the source of our nighttime images? And what is their significance? This is a riddle indeed, and yet I have heard dreaming described as "the secret code to human personality."

Why—if true—is this idea so intriguing? As human beings, we have not been notably successful in understanding ourselves—even though our scientific advances are many. The deepest mystery we still face is our own baffling behavior. We grope desperately for some insight into our own species, and we look hopefully to those who investigate the inner workings of the human mind.

Included among this group of seekers are those who study sleep and dreams. They search the changing states of the sleeping brain for clues that will explain our waking thoughts, feelings, and behavior. They deal with memory and mood, learning and concentration, emotion and creativeness.

Many probe the content of dreams, focusing especially on that familiar star of the nighttime stage, the dreamer's own self. What can that character tell us about our true natures? Is it possible that studying our sleeping selves may help us function better awake; deal with conflict, fear, and rage; enrich ourselves as people?

We can hardly ignore a byway of our lives so promising, so strewn with clues to our true selves. Yet we are confronted at once with a mountain of dream lore heaped up by generations of dreamers. This ancient debris includes countless legends, rumors, mystical beliefs, and fanatical superstitions.

Can we pass quickly through this rubble, pausing only to cull a few useful facts from the fables? If we are ever going to make sense out of dreaming, we'll have to leave the nonsense behind.

Prophets, Poets, and Power Seekers

2

I, Nebuchadnezzar, . . . saw a dream which made me afraid. . . . Therefore made I a decree to bring in all the wise men of Babylon before me, that they might make known unto me the interpretation of the dream.

—Book of Daniel

"May the dream that I dream be favorable," prayed the ancient Babylonian to the goddess of the night. "May the dream that I dream be true." This common prayer says much about how many people throughout the ages have felt about their dreams. They were regarded as omens, warnings, prophecies. Supposedly, they might be messages from demons or gods, from persons absent or dead. People responded to their own dreams out of pious faith, and sometimes out of fear and folly.

The Cheyenne Indians of the Great Plains sent each young boy into a period of fasting and prayer on some lonely butte, there to seek a dream vision of his own destiny. The Egyptian of old who dreamed of sawing wood was thereby assured that his enemies would soon die. In the Holy Book of Islam it is written that the truest dreams are those of good tidings. And in ancient Hungary, there were many who believed that if the dreamer saw himself in a velvet robe, he would soon be blessed with riches.

Men and women searched their dreams for prophecy. In some regions of the world it was believed that at night the soul left the body to range widely in the search. And what if a dreamer was wakened before the soul returned? One shuddered at the thought.

There is probably no religion in the world that does not have its own dream lore. Holy writ is full of tales of the prophetic visions that men and women saw in their sleep. In every era and in every culture, dreams have reported the arrival of gods or humans who would save the world. Out of such dreams, religious societies have been built. Many of their sacred writings contain long lists of various kinds of dreams and their meanings. The Old and New Testaments tell and interpret the night visions of Joseph and Jacob as well as the dreams of the Christian saints and prophets.

Along with their hopes of foreseeing the future, the ancients devoutly believed that dreams would cure their bodily ills. In China, Assyria, and the Pacific Islands are the ruins of shrines where the diseased and crippled came in search of dream cures. From the earliest moments of dawn, they prayed fervently for a healing dream. Then at night they lay down in the dark shadows of the temple, hoping that a vision in sleep would relieve their suffering.

In Borneo, the members of the Ibans tribe believed that a "secret helper" with great powers, a *ngarong*, would reveal himself in a dream. Usually arising from the spirit of a dead relative, the helper might take on almost any form in waking life.

Individuals or groups have often obeyed the messages they found in their dreams. Some dug wells at particular places, or brought sacrifices to temples, or began battles at certain hours. Some drank bitter potions or gave their new-

Enigma by Odilon Redon, Courtesy of the Art Institute of Chicago, Stickney Collection

the prophetic soul
Of the wide world, dreaming on things to come.

—William Shakespeare, *Sonnets* CVII

born children strange names. Instructions that had come to them in their sleep were deeply believed.

Did people find that they could rely on their dreams for good advice? Probably not. But rather than question their dreams, they might blame themselves if something went wrong. Perhaps they had not carried out the instructions properly, or did not understand the dream's meaning. Perhaps they did not deserve the promised rewards.

Although each dream is the vision of a single person, so-called official dreams were said to express the hopes of an entire nation or a group. They were especially powerful when reported by some monarch or high priest. In fact, little attention was ever paid to the sleep visions of the poor and lowly. On the other hand, the glorious dreams of rulers have changed the destinies of nations.

The account of a dream comes to us without proof. And who can say whether the teller is an innocent dreamer or a wakeful schemer? Often dreams have been used as instruments of power.

In Arab legend, there is the story of a pregnant woman who claimed that in a dream she saw herself giving birth to a lion. The beast emerged with a defiant roar, she said, beating the ground with its tail. Then other lions gathered around him, crouching low and bowing their heads. The son who was born to this ambitious woman did in fact become caliph, ruling with great strength and authority.

In the year 1066, as our school books tell us, William the Conqueror invaded England from Normandy. In 1067, William's mother said that when she was giving birth to her notable son, she dreamed that a great tree grew out of her body and spread its branches across the sea. Was the invasion of England, then, an act of aggression? Or was it the fulfillment of a divine prophecy?

Browse through the histories of nations and find how often dreams have been used for good purposes and for evil ones. Often, in the past, dreams have controlled people's lives. Surprisingly, a great many people still look to ancient dogmas to explain their dreams.

SIGN SEEKING

At a corner bookstall in Hong Kong or Dallas or Stockholm or Accra, you should be able to pick up a dream book for a small amount of money. Much in demand, they are always in stock. Dream books have common sources which are thousands of years old. Most are simply modernized versions of books sold over the centuries in the most ancient of cities.

A dream book of classical Rome stated that a dream about a blossoming tree was a prediction of gladness and prosperity. A volume that you can buy at many American newsstands today repeats that such a dream promises "fulfillment of hopes and desires." Ancient Hebrew writings warn that it is unlucky to dream of an owl. Today's dream book says: "To see an owl (in a dream) foretells that you will be secretly maligned and be in danger from enemies."

The ancients were aware that persons, places, and things seen in dreams may represent other persons, places, or things. The dream, they said, is full of symbols that stand for something in our waking lives. The common dream book is a kind of dictionary of symbols, listing objects and happenings seen in dreams, and explaining what they supposedly represent.

Milk is knowledge; a key means change; hair is worry; an arrow is pleasure; cats are bad luck; pins mean quarreling; iron is power; cheese is disappointment; a sneeze denotes a change in plans; a clock is danger; bread is happiness; a steeple predicts sickness; a thread signifies a road and the course of life. And so it goes. Through the ages, the notions of what dreams may signify have not changed very much. In fact, we still have remnants from this ancient vocation—the interpreters of dreams.

From the seers and soothsayers of old have descended many of today's professional tipsters, prophets, and wizards who deal in dreams. The old idea that the gods speak to us in our slumber has been revived by leaders of a number of modern cults and is exploited by fakers, swindlers, and faddists. One such spokesman claims that dreams reveal how to profit on the stock market or at the horse races. Supposedly dream messages cure people of diseases, put them in touch with dead relatives, tell them where to find lost objects, predict the outcome of political elections.

As in so many other forms of fortune-telling, the dream prophecies are familiar ones. You will go on a trip, meet a stranger, receive something of value. Any or all of these forecasts could hardly fail to come true during the course of a lifetime. Another message that is supposedly sent to us through dreams is the omen of death—our own or someone else's. Such was the strange dream of Abraham Lincoln.

It was very late when the president went wearily to bed. This was April 1865. Lincoln had served his country through the agony of the Civil War, now at its close.

Sleep quickly released his mind from the great and small cares of a momentous time. But soon a disturbing dream began: It seemed to the president that he heard sorrowing voices, the wail of lamenting mourners. Lincoln rose from his bed and wandered through the White House, puzzled by the piteous sobbing that grew louder. At length he entered the East Room. To his surprise, it was filled with weeping throngs. Soldiers in uniform solemnly stood guard near a coffin.

"Who is dead in the White House?" Lincoln demanded of one of the guardsmen.

"The president," came the reply. "He was killed by an assassin!"

When Lincoln recounted this dream to friends a few days later, he added, "Then came a loud burst of grief from the crowd, which awoke me from my dreams. I slept no more that night. . . ."

Within days, Lincoln was dead—the victim of an assassin's bullet.

Such stories are told in support of the notion that dreams do, in fact, foretell the future. However, the warning may not be quite as surprising or supernatural as it may seem. In Lincoln's case, he was well aware of his many personal and political enemies. He had, in fact, received no less than eighty threats against his life in that spring of 1865.

"I know I am in danger," Lincoln repeatedly told his associates who urged him to be careful, "but I am not going to worry over threats like these."

Perhaps, in reality, Lincoln was more concerned than he

himself realized. The worry that he dismissed in wakefulness returned to trouble his sleep.

People experience joy in their dreams, and sorrow as well. They may see themselves mirrored in their night visions in many ways. Sometimes dreams may show people as they truly are in wakefulness—or as they would like to be. In other dreams, the self may appear as sinister and hateful.

A startling self-image loomed up in the dreams of Plato, the philosopher of ancient Greece. "In all of us, even in good men," he commented, "there is a lawless wild-beast nature, which peers out in sleep."

WHAT IS REAL?

In the dark, early hours of an August morning in 1885, Robert Louis Stevenson was roused from a terrible nightmare. His outcries in sleep had alarmed his wife, who then shook him awake.

Angrily, the Scottish author mumbled a few unkind words. He was, he said, in the throes of a strange, gripping story. And he complained that it was interrupted before its ending. In the next three days, Stevenson worked like fury, setting down the tale that had unfolded itself in his dream.

This was the story of a respected doctor who changed periodically into a murderous monster. It was published as *The Strange Case of Dr. Jekyll and Mr. Hyde.* Stevenson's shocking tale was to bring him worldwide fame. In its powerful symbol of a person leading a double life, the dream story seemed to be asking some disturbing questions about the nature of human personality.

In the oldest records of humankind, we have shown a driving curiosity about our own nature. Who are we? What is the reality of ourselves? Do we know our true selves, or only what we seem to be?

As human beings we have been fascinated with the notion that none of us are as simple as we appear to be. There is more to us than meets the eye. And nothing is more intriguing to us than the idea of the "other self," the one that may be revealed to us in our dreams.

The dream has itself been used as a symbol in literature. In Washington Irving's story "Rip Van Winkle," the main character's twenty-year sleep and his strange awakening may just be another way of describing the tricks played on us by the passing of time. Rip Van Winkle's slumber has added meaning when we note that twenty years is about the duration of our total sleep during an average lifetime. It is also true that in our dreams we not only leap across space and time, but we also defy the ordinary rules of reason and mix up illusion and reality.

In olden China lived the philosopher Chuang-tzu. He wrote: "Once upon a time, I, Chuang-tzu, dreamt I was a butterfly . . . fluttering hither and thither, to all intents and purposes a butterfly. Suddenly I awaked, and there I lay, myself again. Now, I do not know whether I was a man dreaming I was a butterfly, or whether I am now a butterfly dreaming I am a man."

The land of dreams has always been home for such creative people—those who are rich in imagination and free in fancy. Poet, painter, music maker, dancer—these are folk who are often called dreamers. And whether they dream by day or by night, they seem comfortable in the dreamlike state. Like the Chinese sage, they may move back and forth easily between a real existence and a realm of fantasy, making few distinctions between the two. The playwright or the filmmaker is a builder of scenes—illusions that are sometimes little different from dreams. And dreams, like imaginative paintings, are visual and graphic. The poet, too, works with imagery, symbols, and metaphors. And according to students of dream content, these are exactly the elements comprising dreams.

As readers, many of us are charmed by stories that are dreamlike. *Alice in Wonderland,* the Oz stories, *The Hobbit—* these are the works of writers whose domain is fantasy. They fashion a total world of make-believe. The spell they cast is made out of reverie and whimsy, gibberish and poppycock. It is preposterous nonsense, yet we are delighted enough to seek in it some deeper meaning.

The dream is a private, intimate web we ourselves have woven. In design, size, shape, and color, it is our very own thing! The strands contain assorted bits and pieces woven into place—a scrap of fluff from some childhood memory, a thread of fear we have never escaped, a toy we once cherished, a hurtful word spoken thoughtlessly, a wave of farewell to a special person, a horse that once whinnied softly in our ear.

For many of us, our dreams are perhaps our best artistic efforts. We can create nighttime masterpieces of the imagination that might forever be viewed with awe and wonder—if the world could only see them!

A SOURCE OF IDEAS

The stuff of dreams is clearly not limited to moonbeams and gossamer and fairy dust. And it is not the creative artist alone who draws useful material from the illusions of the night.

In countless recorded instances, people have been guided by their dreams in solving practical problems. Asleep or awake, half-asleep or half-awake, the mind continues to function in some fashion. The dream, the nightmare, the day-dream—each often produces useful images that have eluded us in full wakefulness.

Many inventors have seen, during slumber, the answer to puzzles that wearied their waking minds. Some of the great thinkers of the past have stirred from sleep or drowsiness with fresh and powerful concepts. Many of us have had the experience of going to bed with a knotty problem and some-how finding the answer long before morning.

In the middle of the nineteenth century, an American, Elias Howe, invented a sewing machine. The details of this device came to him in a dream.

In the winter of 1912, the Danish physicist, Niels Bohr, worked at a feverish pace on the remaining baffling questions that would at last explain the structure of the atom. The scientist was oblivious to night or day, sleep or wakefulness, and in a bright flash of enlightenment, the correct answer finally roused him one February morning.

Similarly, Albert Einstein made one of his greatest dis-coveries at a time when he was too ill to work in his laboratory. Feverish and exhausted, he lay on his sickbed, half-dozing. Suddenly he awoke, the theory of relativity clearly outlined in his mind.

Dreams and science—what a strange pair of bedfellows! One is systematic and rational, the other random and fanciful. Our dreams come to us unplanned and unbidden; our scientific efforts are the results of much preparation, skill, and knowledge.

Oddly, these two contrasting modes of thought have now been brought together in quite an unexpected way. Within recent years, our view of dreaming has changed completely from what it was throughout our entire history.

Undoubtedly, our earliest human ancestors awoke from startling sleep visions and wondered about their sources or meanings. That kind of speculation about dreams continued almost unchanged throughout the centuries. The long era was filled with uncertainty, supposition, fantasy, and heresay. Until recent years, the dream remained completely outside the bounds of genuine knowledge. Around it were spun beliefs, opinions, and theories that could neither be proved nor disproved.

Up until the 1950s, the pondering of dreams had yielded nothing that could possibly be observed, measured, or verified by reasonable or scientific methods. No single fact about dreams could be firmly stated other than the general truth that human beings do dream.

But something happened on the South Side of Chicago in the spring of 1952—an event that was to put the dreamer into the scientific laboratory and condemn many a scientist to sleepless nights!

Eyes in the Night

3

"He's dreaming now," said Tweedledee,
"and what do you think he's dreaming about?"
Alice said, "Nobody can guess that."

—Lewis Carroll, *Alice in Wonderland*

Both the nurses and the newborn babies had become accustomed to the slender young student in the white coat. Eugene Aserinsky had made himself a familiar figure in the nursery of the big hospital near the University of Chicago campus. That was where he spent his sleepless nights, making tedious observations, recording on his chart every movement, yawn, sneeze, and outcry.

Aserinsky was deeply absorbed in a study of the patterns of infant sleep. Much of what this serious young man had to report to the director of this research, Professor Nathaniel Kleitman, was routine. But one of his nighttime observations was not.

As he watched one sleeping baby, he noted how the infant's eyes moved under the closed lids. Was he seeing things? The student adjusted his eyeglasses and blinked in astonishment. He then watched the other babies more closely.

Throughout that night he observed periods of similar eye movements in each of the infants. He could hardly wait until morning to report his discovery.

During the next few nights, Eugene Aserinsky made a detailed check of the behavior of the slumbering infants. He found that each child spent an initial period getting settled into sleep—stretching, blinking, kicking, turning, making faces. But after a time, bodily activity decreased. Then the eyeballs could be seen rolling up and down and side to side under the closed eyelids. Gradually, the eye movement became more rapid.

The duration of the eye activity varied for each child. What followed was a quiescent period. But somewhat later in the night the twitching seen on the closed eyes signaled that the eyeballs had once again become active.

Aserinsky carefully recorded the periods of eye movement. They recurred many times during the sleeping period. On succeeding nights he detected the same behavior for every infant. Within a week, he had an accurate record—the first of its kind ever made.

Aserinsky knew that he had come upon an important discovery, and he could only guess at its full meaning. But such a guess—call it a theory or a hypothesis—is an important part of any scientific work and forms the framework for further research.

Together with Kleitman, Aserinsky set out to prove or disprove a series of hypotheses:

1. Rapid eye movements are activities common to all sleeping human beings.
2. The periods of eye movement are periods of dreaming.
3. The occurrence of dream periods throughout the night can be scientifically verified.

The first experiments with sleeping adult volunteers quickly confirmed that rapid eye movement was part of the common sleeping behavior of everyone. And researchers had startling news for those who showed up in their lab and announced that they never dreamed. Awakened during eye movement periods, such volunteers readily poured out vivid dream accounts. There were no nondreamers—only dreamers who could not remember their dreams the morning after!

On the average, the research showed, people have four or five dreams every night. They occur at intervals of about ninety minutes. What is the duration of dreams? They vary, it was learned. The first dream of the night is rather short. The last dream is a full-length experience. Usually complete with sound, color, excitement, and a full cast of characters, this early morning dream is often a tangled, complicated story, sometimes made up of many separate scenes.

These bursts of jerky movement in closed, unseeing eyes could not be explained. But it was certain that they accompanied every full-fledged dream. As if the mysteries of dreaming were not already enough—now this weird phenomenon!

During the summer and autumn of 1952, the lab in Chicago eagerly pursued every fresh trail stemming from that first find. A new field of research had been opened. And soon the world at large would take notice. The discovery made by an observant student in a baby ward was to awaken anew all the age-old curiosities about the nature of sleep and dreams.

The news from the University of Chicago quickly roused those few scholars and scientists who had been patiently puzzling over the night life of our species. On the Chicago campus, the scientific breakthrough attracted a fresh crop of avid students to the field of sleep and dreams. They set about learning a new way to learn about dreams, and soon, the Chicago campus spawned a strange breed of sleepy people whose nights were spent watching others sleep.

One of these, William C. Dement, was to tag an everlasting name to the motion of eyeballs during slumber. This activity became known as rapid eye movement, REM for short.

BRAIN WAVES

William C. Dement emerged as one of the more durable of the sleep-dream scientists. From 1957 until now he has continued a tireless probe into the secrets of slumber.

Today, this bluff, hearty scholar may be found at California's Stanford University, running a large experimental lab and a clinic that deals with sleep disorders. Patients come to him with a thousand problems of the night, as well as uncontrollable tendencies to doze off in the midst of an active day. In Dement's lab, I found his research team working with several poodles who strangely collapse into sleep—often in the middle of a meal!

Across twenty years, Dement has monitored thousands of dreams. He has experimented with sleeplessness and dreamlessness, tried to influence the visions of dreamers, tested the sending of dream messages, and worked with such dreamers as drug addicts, sleepwalkers, the mentally ill, nightmare sufferers, snorers, and creative people who solve problems in their sleep.

Since the 1950s, Dement has brilliantly carried on the work begun by Kleitman and Aserinsky. There was great excitement in those early days about the new discoveries, and there were high hopes as to where they might lead. Dement added much to the spirit of inquiry and quest. He also proved to be expert in using the newfangled tools of sleep research.

Great leaps in scientific achievement have to do largely with people and their inspired ideas. But often the pace of scientific advancement depends on the availability of the right kinds of tools. Galileo's bold theories about the heavens could be proved only because the newly invented telescope was at hand. Medical progress moved forward with the discovery of X rays. Space science needed electronic telemetry.

The scientific work on sleep and dreams relied strongly on a wired box called the electroencephalograph. The word breaks down into three parts: *electro* ("electric"); *encephalo* ("brain"); *graph* ("writing").

This remarkable device was first used for diagnosing diseases of the brain. It amplifies and records weak electrical currents that flow continuously across the living brain. These so-called brain waves can be detected without making direct contact with the brain itself. The flow of energy is picked up painlessly from tabs attached to the head. Fine wires from these electrodes carry the impulses into the machine.

A long finger, tipped with a pen, writes the message from the machine onto a moving strip of paper. The writing is a continuous line made by the up-and-down movements of the pen. The zigzags reveal the speeds, strengths, and types of brain signals. This is a record that can easily be understood by anyone who is trained to "read" the electroencephalogram, or EEG as it is called.

It was just such a machine that was wheeled into the University of Chicago lab. The early experiments put this sensitive EEG machine to a severe test: Could dream time be precisely recorded and measured by electronic methods? Was REM the only true indicator of dreaming? Could REM become the means of building a vast and systematic collection of dreams?

The early research successes spurred new experiments. Human volunteers for the Chicago sleep lab were not easy to find. But Dement, still a graduate student, turned out to be a persuasive recruiter. He lured students, housewives, and jobless workers to nightly employment. The pay was not much, but then the only work was sleeping on the job!

During the long nights that followed, an astounding mass of data was accumulated. REM awakenings yielded an enormous number of dreams, several from each volunteer in a single night. By simply stirring a REM sleeper, researchers were practically guaranteed a fresh and detailed dream report!

Another part of the experiment was to rouse sleepers at times when there were no REM indications on the EEG machine. These awakenings produced few recollections of full-blown dreams.

The EEG machine, recording brain waves, was capable of detecting other ongoing body functions as well. In fact, the machine was now writing its reports with a row of pens, producing tracings that showed simultaneous activity of various parts of the body during sleep.

In addition to the movements of the eyes, the changing state of the muscular system was measurable by the EEG. At the same time, heart rate, blood pressure, and breathing records were made. The sleeper could be "wired for sound," and checked for changes on the surface of the skin or in the chemistry within the organs. In time, the term REM came to mean not merely eye movement but the entire complex of body functions that accompany this state of sleep.

Some experiments with the EEG machine provoked more questions than answers. It was Dement who discovered REM sleep in cats. Dreaming cats? If so, what images might enliven feline sleep?

In a brief time, scientific research shattered some of the oldest and most popular notions about dreams. Completely destroyed were these old ideas:

1. Most people seldom dream, and many do not dream at all.
2. Dreams rarely occur more than once in a night.
3. During sleep, the brain, like a switched-off machine, ceases to function.
4. Dreams last only a few seconds.

Dement showed that the dream occurs in "real time." In other words, the events in the dream last about as long as the same events would take if they were acted out in a waking state.

Dement and a growing number of researchers in this

new scientific field spent sleepless nights in the sleep lab. They scanned the telltale EEG reports from each of the bedrooms where volunteers slumbered. For Dement, these long nights were a time for pondering unanswered questions: Why do we dream? How much dream time do we need? Are the darting eyes of the sleepers actually watching the dream? Do dreams occur *only* during REM periods? Dement was still in the dark.

TRIALS AND ERRORS

The early years that brought dream study into the scientific laboratory were like one long Fourth of July with explosive new discoveries flaring in the murky night.

But not all the experiments were successful. Some fizzled. Promising lines of research led only to disappointing results. Overly eager experimenters announced findings that were later disproved.

From several laboratories came word that dreamers' eye movements could be matched with their dream stories. One dreamer whose eyes moved back and forth was watching a tennis game, it was claimed. Another dreamer with up-and-down eye movements was dreaming of climbing a ladder, or tossing free throws into a basketball hoop.

Alas, these reports proved to be misleading. Hundreds of other dream reports were checked. In most cases, the dream content had nothing at all to do with the pace or direction in which the dreamer's eyes moved.

At one point, the announcement was made that people

who are blind from birth do not have rapid eye movements. It was not long afterward that this finding was completely overturned by new research.

Some experiments sought to discover the effects of sleep loss. And these studies revealed, once again, one of the hazards faced by scientists setting out in a new field of research—experiment results are not always what they seem.

Early studies indicated that the continuous loss of sleep would necessarily result in serious and permanent mental disorders. Then in 1965 came the case of Randy Gardner, a San Diego high school student who had decided to break the world's record for going without sleep. Randy remained awake through eleven days and nights, finally breaking the sleepless record at 264 hours. A day or two later, Randy had caught up on his sleep needs and was back to normal. Certainly, Randy Gardner was an unusual case with remarkable physical fitness and stamina, and few could even attempt such a feat without ill effects. However, sleep researchers were compelled to revise some previous conclusions about the dire results of sleep loss.

Another scientific controversy raged around the simple question: What is a dream? The answers differed. For some, dreams were the storylike episodes experienced by sleeping persons. Another view was that dreaming includes any and all mental activity during sleep. A third opinion maintained that a dream is whatever images appear in the mind during REM periods.

Electronic monitoring of the brain cells confirmed what many had long suspected—our mental activity is as continuous as is blood circulation, breathing, or heartbeat.

Clearly, the brain at bedtime does not simply quit for the night. Instead, the brain cells continue to "fire" at varying rates, producing signals of different voltages on the electroencephalogram.

NREM (non-REM) periods are recorded as quieter sleep, with slow, low-voltage waves predominating on the EEG readout. With the onset of REM sleep, the brain shifts to another mode. Activity is heightened. The brain cells fire at high rates, sometimes with even greater frequency than during wakefulness.

However, these differences in brain waves could not entirely settle the definition of the dream. The EEG machine can supply no clue as to the images being produced in the sleeper's mind. This information can only come from inquiry with human subjects aroused from sleep at moments coinciding with various readings on the EEG record. Such studies showed marked differences between the mental activities of NREM and REM periods.

NREM arousals often brought an unclear response from the sleeper. If the sleeper reported anything at all, it was a kind of mulling, wandering, drifting remembrance of half-formed ideas rather than visual images. It was as though the sleeper was reviewing a series of vague notions—shadowy reflections of daytime thought.

By contrast, the REM dream, particularly the last one of the night, usually has the full quality of an actual experience. Lifelike scenes are featured, catching the dreamer up in a series of real events. The active REM dream is frequently filled with strong feelings, the dreamer weathering intense emotional storms.

Cyclops by William Baziotes, Courtesy of the Art Institute of Chicago, Walter M. Campana Memorial Purchase Prize

The eye of man hath not heard, the ear of man hath not seen, man's hand is not able to taste, his tongue to conceive, nor his heart to report, what my dream was.

—William Shakespeare,
A Midsummer Night's Dream IV.i.

NREM recollections are dreams of a kind. But the REM dream, with all its imaginative complexity, is the product of a high level of mental activity. The sleeping brain remains continuously at work. The dream is its brainchild.

STATES AND STAGES

"Pleasant REMs!" That's what they say at bedtime in the San Diego home of Laverne Johnson. He is the sleep expert for the U. S. Navy and a sharp-minded student of dreams.

My talks with him centered on the threefold lives we seem to lead—waking, sleeping, and dreaming. Johnson quickly leafed through a stack of round-the-clock EEG reports, taken from volunteers during both their sleeping and waking hours. He pointed to some startling similarities between the brain waves of wakefulness and dreaming.

But what about the non-REM state which takes up the longest periods of our sleep? Is sleep *deeper* at certain hours of the night? Are there times when we are more easily aroused? Is NREM a steady, uniform pattern of sleep?

As NREM sleep appears on the EEG record, four distinct stages may be seen. Stage 1 is sleep onset, which ordinarily appears in full form only once, during the first hour. Then NREM Stages 2, 3, and 4 follow in succession. Each differs in wave patterns from the others, and the entire first half of the night is normally dominated by the slow-wave sleep of Stage 4. The second half of the night is when most of the REM sleep occurs.

The four NREM stages may begin as a series, followed

by the first brief REM period. But after this first cycle, NREM stages reappear in random fashion in between the REM periods.

"Let's not forget that the stages of sleep are a man-made invention," cautions Johnson. And he adds that we do not yet know what bodily needs are met by each stage.

Johnson's talk about need and arousal pointed us toward some of the deepest questions that are yet to be answered. In what ways are sleep and dreams connected with the survival and preservation of life? In what stages of sleep is the human being or any other sleeping animal most safe, most responsive to a warning signal, most sensitive to danger?

"Sleep is not unconsciousness, and outside stimuli do get through to your brain," Johnson commented. "But you do turn off the insignificant signals and are responsive to the important ones."

Research has shown that a sleeper is most easily aroused by whatever signal has a personal meaning. The best example is that of parents who may sleep soundly through a noisy thunderstorm but awaken at the first faint cry of their baby.

In the sleep lab in San Diego, Navy personnel, both asleep and awake, have been scientifically tested for their responses to various signals—to tones mechanically produced and finely controlled. In this research, the term *deep sleep* has proved to be rather meaningless.

If "depth" in sleep stages is measured by how readily the sleeper may be aroused, research shows us no sharp contrasts. People are awakened somewhat more easily from REM and Stage 1 and 2 sleep than from Stages 3 and 4, but the differences are not great. Arousal levels are related more to individual responses than to distinct sleep stages. There are also few indications that some stages of sleep are markedly deeper than others in providing rest and overcoming fatigue. From his work with Navy people, Johnson points out that "changing the relative amounts of time spent in each sleep stage does not appear to affect wakeful behavior very much."

Johnson typifies what is special about many of the scientists working on sleep and dreams. He bridges the gap between psychology and physiology, the two main viewpoints from which this field of study is usually approached. Laverne Johnson began his professional career as a psychologist, a student of human behavior and the mind. However, he also became deeply interested in the workings of the brain—its structure, functions, chemistry, and physiology. Brain and mind are the double focus of today's sleep and dream research.

Restless and probing intelligence keeps any science fresh and free from stagnation. It is one sign of the healthy condition of sleep-dream science that some of its researchers are always asking the "tough questions"—questions like those posed by Johnson and two of his associates, Paul Naitoh and Ardie Lubin. The latter is a stocky, gray-bearded scientist who brings wide experience and a lot of good humor to his work.

In a lively interchange, we talked about the many controversies surrounding sleep and dreams. Lubin is concerned about the common use of sleep-inducing pills "that only create more insomnia." And he scoffs at those who claim to be able to help people stop smoking or overeating, or to learn a foreign language or calculus by means of tape recordings played during slumber.

Fortunately for Johnson and his associates, the Navy is in need of information as to the effects of sleep loss and fatigue, the sleep habits of submarine crews, and the problems of jet pilots streaking across time zones. It therefore affords rich opportunities for scientific work. However, the sleep lab at San Diego is not limited to exploring the special nighttime behavior of Navy personnel.

The scientists here have also contributed a good deal to the general field of sleep-dream research. To the EEG they have added the effective use of computers. They have also modeled new electronic skills that are now widely used. Many of these techniques have been added to that central core of modern research—the sleep lab.

Science and Sleep 4

For some must watch, while some must sleep.
—William Shakespeare, *Hamlet* III.ii.

Early in the sleety winter night, we arrive to set up the experiment. Our four echoing voices are the only sounds in the Behavioral Sciences Building on the University of Illinois' Circle Campus. The talk is casual, but anxious—the conversation of people about to tap into other people's dreams.

Rosalind Cartwright, the director of this research, leads us through a "hardware checkout" of sleeping rooms, intercoms, EEG machines, tape recorders, supplies. The control room of the sleep lab is like a kind of spaceship just before lift-off, with one difference—they, not we in the capsule, are "taking off."

I run through a checklist of the do's and don'ts of laboratory procedure. The fountain pens on the EEG machines are unusually skittish tonight, like a row of racehorses at the starting gate. Before they all behave, there is much purple ink spilled and some purple language used. One of the intercoms has a bad switch that must be repaired, and the EEG machines are fed with a quarter mile of folded graph paper. The electronic circuits are put through a dry run.

There is an hour or more of thorough testing and inspection before our student volunteers arrive. The four—Kim, Harry, Marty, Joan—display a full range of feelings, from nervous and dubious, to confident and cool. In the first nights of a sleep experiment, unusual attitudes, behavior, and sleep patterns are expected.

Our subjects get ready for bed. They are each assigned a small sleeping cubicle which is "bugged" for sound and electronic monitoring. In turn, they each submit to the ritual of getting hooked up. This is tricky work. By the time they are ready, they will be living transmitters. Eight electrodes are being attached to each volunteer. First, a braid of wires, held in place with a piece of gauze soaked in sticky collodion, is fastened to the head. The small wires are color coded for placement—two to the outside edge of each eye, two behind the ears, two on the scalp, two to the forehead. Now these circuits are checked. The tester sends through a tingle of electric current if contact is being made with the right tissues.

Marty has brought a favorite blanket. Joan asks wistfully for a bedtime story but is joshed out of it as conduct unbecoming a college senior. Harry's tensions will show up later in an almost sleepless night.

"Lights out!" Plugged in, the four immediately begin sending EEG waves. The folds of paper are now moving steadily through the machine, a minute per double fold. The quivering pens are writing in a cramped but even script; except for the eye records which show the slow wandering visual patterns of people trying to settle down for the night in strange surroundings. Dr. Cartwright identifies the brain report as "pretty alpha waves," typical of relaxed, wakeful thought.

Kim drowses off first. She will sleep steadily throughout

the night, except for those REM periods of early morning when she will be summoned awake to report on her dreams. Marty will prove to be an equally steady sleeper. Joan is to spend a fitful night.

This is an experiment in color telepathy. During the second half of the night, we experimenters will draw one sheet of colored paper at random from a bag containing paper of many colors. We will then "send" this color to the sleepers during the first portions of REM periods merely by concentrating hard on the chosen color. "Think pink," is the way Dr. Cartwright describes the process. The color actually drawn is green.

When awakened, each sleeper will be asked: "What was going on in your mind when we called you? Were there any colors of objects, people, or backgrounds? What colors?"

But the night is still young, and we settle down for the long watch. We're taking bets on who REMs first. Someone remarks, "You get a little seasick watching these waves hour after hour."

It is quiet. The fountain pens scratch, the coffee pot slurps. Sleep sounds come through the loudspeakers as our students thrash around in their beds, snore gently, yawn audibly. Tension builds as we wait for the first erratic waves of REM. . . .

THE DREAM MAKER

Can I invade your dream, or you enter mine? Or is dreamland a private and forbidden zone marked "No Trespassing?"

Our small-scale experiment in transmitting color to

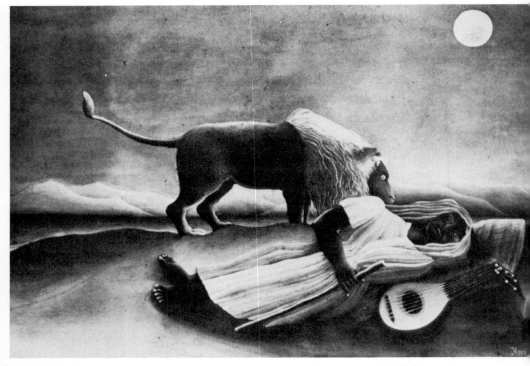

The Sleeping Gypsy by Henri Rousseau, Collection, The Museum of Modern Art, New York

Was it a vision, or a waking dream?
Fled is that music:—do I wake or sleep?

—John Keats, *Ode to a Nightingale*

dreaming minds was a modest success. One of our subjects dreamed of watching two people trying to train a dog to fetch and carry a (green) watermelon. Two others received a "green message," though it was much less strong.

On a subsequent night, the chosen color was dark brown. Here again, one subject reported a clear vision of only one color—the randomly selected one. Through his drowsy stupor, this student mumbled about the "rich brown earth" that had colored his dream. "Spooky!" Cartwright called it.

What did we learn from this experiment, if anything? Only that there was much more work ahead of us on dream telepathy. Perhaps thousands of additional tests might give us a fragment of a tentative result.

It is two decades now since Dement and others did their early experiments in influencing dreams by external stimuli. They bombarded sleepers with a variety of sensations—spraying cold water on their bare skin, playing music, flashing lights, ringing bells. Other experiments tried to influence dream patterns by preparing subjects before bed for a variety of nighttime discomforts. Some were fed salty foods, others were shown disturbing films, and still others were filled with great amounts of liquid to induce bladder tension.

All this meddling with dreams produced few results. Dreams, it seems, cannot be created by anyone but the dreamer—although outside influences may at times become part of a dream in progress. As Dement put it. "Stimuli may modify an ongoing dream, but do not initiate it."

But what if a window shutter should bang in the night, or a spicy sausage eaten before bedtime should set one's stomach rumbling? What if a train howls in the distance, or the bedroom becomes sticky warm? Wouldn't these necessarily become part of the dream? People who have studied such things say it is unlikely.

A research group at New York University once sent a group of eighteen volunteers to bed in a thirsty state. During the night, a tape recorded message murmured to each of them about a "cool, delicious drink of water." In the morning, a few recalled having dreams about thirst and water. However, a good many similar efforts at penetrating dream content were not nearly as successful.

In another test, groups of volunteers were shown several kinds of films just before bedtime each night for a week. What turned up in their dreams? A romantic comedy had not the slightest effect. A Western movie with lots of fist-fighting and gunplay seemed to bring on animated and stressful night visions. However, in no case did the actual story material of the films show up in any of the volunteers' reported dreams.

Here we see what is meant by the "third state," a kind of existence during dreams that is different from both quiet sleep and wakefulness. While awake, our senses, nerves, brains, and muscular systems are coordinated in a smooth, rapid flow that results in continuous responses to stimuli. When a stoplight turns red, the driver reacts.

During dreaming, many stimuli also occur. Some are external. Others are experienced as part of the dream vision. However, in neither case does the body respond to these stimuli as it does during wakefulness.

Experimentation with animals has given us some clues

as to the nature of this "third state." These studies assume that animals do dream. Since animals can give us no account of their mental activity, we can only use the term *dream* very loosely when applied to nonhuman species. However, there is increasing experimental evidence that animals do have dream images of some kind.

It was the brilliant research directed by Michel Jouvet in France that revealed some of the most dramatic aspects of this "third state." Jouvet has carried on an intensive search for the chemistry and brain structures that are involved in dreamlike processes. His lab has worked with cats that have been deprived of the major portions of their brains. Devoid of their cerebral cortices, these cats still proved to be fully capable of having REM periods during sleep.

The research in France studied the changes in muscular activity during the REM state. The onset of REM is signaled by the shutoff of the body's motor system. The cat's neck and back muscles go completely limp, and all gross movements of the animal cease. Jouvet was able to locate the center in the brain which triggers this shutoff of muscles. By destroying cells in this center, Jouvet evoked some startling results. The cat, still asleep and dreaming, suddenly sprang into action. It seemed to be acting out a violent dream. The animal leaped and pounced, and snarled in fear and rage so intense that the experimenter had to back away.

It is this kind of ongoing research that has put sleep visions in a new light. Clearly there are dream processes, more delicate and complex than we ever dreamed of, at work in animals and human beings.

Our dreams are a kind of haunting background music

that seem to give a downbeat to our lives. They are timed to the great rhythms of nature as well.

NINETY MINUTES

Picture the Pacific seaside town of La Jolla and eight people going their everyday ways. They are a teacher, photographer, librarian, store clerk, student, computer operator, technician, and housewife.

As they move about in their separate work—shopping, visiting, loafing—they each carry a small timer that buzzes every ten minutes. At the signal, they stop whatever they are doing and speak into a pocket-size tape recorder to report all their thoughts during the previous ten minutes.

This is an experiment designed by Daniel F. Kripke, who directs the Sleep Diagnostic Laboratory in the big Veterans Hospital in La Jolla. What hypothesis is he testing? What data is he seeking?

Kripke's experiment follows out the known fact that REM periods occur at about ninety-minute intervals throughout the night. "We expect that the mind follows similar rhythms during the day," he told me, "and we are beginning to find that this is true."

Fantasies and daydreams are a part of our normal existence. They occur during our waking hours when someone or something does not control our complete attention. These reveries are most common during periods of resting, boredom, or routine tasks. They are flights of fancy, sometimes as vivid as our most realistic night dreams. Is it surprising that they tend to occur during wakefulness in the same rhythmic patterns as do our nightly dreams?

Some of the work of Kripke and his associates, using more advanced methods and equipment, follows up previous studies by others. One earlier experiment, performed at Mount Sinai Hospital in New York, studied people in a comfortable, well-supplied lounge. Without knowing the nature of the experiment or even that they were being observed, the subjects spent a leisurely day. Records of their food, soft drink, and cigarette intake showed that the high points of these oral activities averaged about ninety minutes apart.

In his work at the La Jolla Veterans Hospital, Kripke has explored many aspects of wakeful behavior that occur in cycles. He is dealing with the ups and downs of our day, the fact that we go through peaks and valleys of efficiency, health, creativeness, alertness, emotion. In what ways are these daytime changes connected with the nightly recurrence of REMs?

Kripke is a sturdy, dark-bearded man with a talent for novel experiments. In studying subjects on a fasting program, he placed balloons inside their stomachs to determine how often they had hunger pangs. He discovered that stomach contractions occur regularly at intervals of about ninety to one hundred minutes.

Some of these experiments opened up unexpected research pathways. A few of Kripke's volunteers did not react according to normal rhythms. On closer examination, these subjects were found to be suffering from deep mental disorders. For Kripke, this finding opened up some new possibilities. He is now conducting a study on the use of "biological rhythm disturbances" to diagnose the problems of mental patients.

It is Daniel Kripke's view that we are governed by combinations of nerve cells and hormones that act as oscillators or pacemakers. "At this point, we are far from being able to map out our day according to our rest and activity cycles," he explains. "But such mapping in the future does not seem farfetched."

The steady tick of a biological clock in all of us is not a new discovery. It has long been known that our bodies are obedient to the sun and the moon. Along with the rest of living nature, we are deeply affected by the patterns of gravity, magnetism, light waves, air pressure. Like fiddler crabs and forest lilies, arctic terns and springtime deer, we react to the wheel of the seasons, the ebb and flow of tides, the clockwork of night and day. Within these larger time scales, we live by the beat of the REM cycle, the rhythm of dreams.

Our closest relatives in the animal world, the large apes, share our REM cycle of about ninety minutes. According to their size, life pattern, development, and metabolism, mammals differ widely in the timing of REMs. REM times range from every nine and a half minutes for a mouse, all the way up to a two-hour interval for an elephant.

Both the animal and human REM cycles vary with age. Young children have a shorter cycle than human adults, and infant REMs may come forty to fifty minutes apart. Elderly people live by slower rhythms, though the average is about ninety minutes. Thus the human REM cycle is neither mechanical nor punctual. Each of us has our individual variations.

How changeable are these patterns? Human subjects have been tested in many ways and in an amazing variety of environments—in outer space, the Arctic regions, high altitudes, undersea, and below the surface of the earth. These experiments confirm the ninety-minute cycle.

In a desolate corner of Alpine France, three young men recently spent five lonely months in a deep cavern. These three spelunkers, or cave explorers, were monitored by instruments in a control station at the mouth of the cave. And though they lived "beyond time," they tried to maintain what they considered to be a normal twenty-four-hour day. Unknown to themselves, they reached a sleeping-waking pattern of forty-eight hours—thirty-four hours awake and fourteen hours asleep. Their previous sense of day and night had vanished. But their ninety-minute REM sleep cycle continued unchanged!

A NEW COMMUNITY

Cave dwellers, electronic engineers, zoologists, and computer specialists are only part of the mix of people to be found in sleep-dream work.

In its brief lifetime, this new field of research has had to create its own scientific community. Its members are as varied as some of the questions they ask: Does the fringe-toed lizard (or any other reptile) have REM sleep? Why do human males regularly have penis erections during REM periods? Do hibernating animals have dreams? What is the effect of drugs on dreams? What can dream research tell us about the two halves of the brain and their different functions? Do sleep disorders cause sudden infant death? How do dreams affect our daytime moods?

These seekers come mainly out of several distinct backgrounds. A good many have their professional roots in physiology and medical science. Others received their education in psychology and the study of behavior. Still another large group are biochemists.

In some respects, the different groups retain their original specialties. But all have crossed over into new studies and reeducated themselves for the many-sided demands of sleep-dream research. Today they are a close-knit professional society working together toward broad, common scientific goals. Meet a few of these men and women who have made a profession of studying sleep and dreams:

Peter Hauri is a hearty, Swiss-born psychologist who lives and works in the gentle New Hampshire hills that surround Dartmouth College. Late one August night we sat in his clinic, pondering the meaning of dreams. "Remember," he pointed out, "you are exactly the same person in your dreams that you are in wakefulness."

In another part of the world, Jean-Louis Valatx is deeply involved "in the search for the gene of sleep and dreams." To this young Frenchman, the dream is a part of our biological heritage from prehuman ancestors—a behavior necessary for their survival, and perhaps for ours as well.

At the University of Illinois, Circle Campus, the dream work is under the capable direction of Rosalind Cartwright, a bright and outreaching teacher and researcher. "The dream deals with the most highly personal material," she says. And while fascinated by dream meanings, she is also keenly aware of the dream state as a body and brain function that can be observed and measured, recorded and analyzed.

On the University of California's huge campus in Los Angeles, Carmine Clemente, a specialist on the nervous system, is one of the young veterans of sleep research. "Sleep occurs in living cells," he reminded me, "and we must never lose sight of the organic basis for it."

Julie Moses is a young researcher whose work on sleep stages is based in the U. S. Navy Hospital at San Diego. Among her interests is sleep arousal. She talks about the strange way a sound sleeper may ignore her completely as she calls out a dozen names—and then pop awake the instant his own name is whispered!

At the University of Chicago, Allan Rechtschaffen directs the dream research. He is a wiry, intense man who relaxes by coiling and re-coiling himself in his big leather chair as he talks. "We spend a third of our lives in the various stages of sleep," he says, "and we don't know why—yet."

Long before I met David Foulkes, I heard his fellow scientists speak with awe of his research. He works with children and their dreams in the mountain town of Laramie, Wyoming, the campus of the state university. Foulkes has a reputation for the boldness of his experiments and the cautiousness of his claims. Yet he expresses high hopes. In probing the sleeping mind, he feels "we may improve our understanding of the mind awake."

That notion is repeated in many forms as the dream researchers talk about their aims. Call it a dream—but these men and women follow a bright inner vision. Their goals explain their attitude toward a kind of work that is round-the-clock, repetitious, and demanding of high skills and ingenuity. Research in this field is often painstaking, wearisome, and without quick or easy rewards. But the long-range promises are extraordinary.

Certainly none of these specialists can tell us where or why dreams are made. As for the inner meaning of a dream, do not expect any two of them to agree.

However, objective information about dreaming does exist. Wise people of stubborn courage, spending their days and nights in the systematic study of dreaming, have set a truth-finding process into motion. There are even some who will now speak in lucid, wakeful moments about a "science of dreams."

The Stuff of Dreams   5

Dreams are not falling apples or visible planets, steaming teakettles or water-worn rocks. Dreams are, in fact, unpromising materials out of which to build a science.

How can the vanishing shadows that cross the slumbering mind be turned into hard scientific facts? Where is the dream data that can stand rigorous testing in controlled experiments with verifiable results? How can dream reports be cleansed of uncertainty and guesswork, freed from personal viewpoints or human sentiments?

The greatest obstacle, of course, is that the dream has no material substance. It is merely a fleeting image in the mind of a single person, the dreamer.

The dream must pass through two filtering processes before it can begin to become a piece of usable information. First, the dreamer must recall the dream. And everyone knows how difficult that can be. Usually only fragments are remembered—disconnected bits and pieces. As a rule, the recollection contains rambling scenes, vague as to beginnings, middles, and endings.

The second process occurs when the dreamer recounts

the dream. How well is it described? How clearly is the memory translated into words? And what unknown feelings may lead the dreamer to withhold information, or change it, or even to falsify it outright?

The reported dream is a thing to be dealt with soberly. It is not "pure" information, but neither is it so suspect as to be worthless. A certain portion of the total data in a large collection of dreams will certainly contain some confusion, error, or falsehood. But it is possible to estimate and discount some reasonable percentage of the total and still be left with a body of useful information. A good many other sciences have to deal with data in the same way.

The discovery of REM in 1952 instantly enriched the quantity and the quality of dream data. The appearance of irregular REM scrawls on the EEG record became clearly recognized as the onset of the dream. Then the researcher had only to wait until the dream ran its course, wake the dreamer, and learn what the mind's eye had seen. For the first time, the dream report was freshly remembered and detailed. Moreover, each night yielded multiple dreams from a single dreamer.

In time, other REM signals were recognized. Cats can sleep with their bodies in a ball, their heads erect. But at REM time, their heads slump downward. The sign of REM in rabbits is the drooping of their pointed ears. In human beings, the appearance of the dream is announced by the sagging of the chin muscle. In some REM research, the drop in muscle tone rather than eye movement is used to signal REM onset.

For the scientist working in this field, the presence or

absence of a dream has been stripped of its bafflement. Although the dream in progress cannot be observed in the laboratory, its existence can be verified by the EEG record, and its duration measured. From this bit of objective data scientists must find some clear patterns of information.

Science is first of all a search for order. The universe, nature, life—all tend to present a vague, haphazard picture until the beginnings of an orderly pattern appear. For example, once we know *when* butterfly migrations, comets, seed sproutings, and eclipses occur, we are better prepared to learn *what* is happening—and *why*. So it is with dreams. Once REM became an observable phenomenon, the scientific method could be applied to the study of dreams.

Whether scientist or lay person, it is the content of dreams that arouses a deep curiosity. By nature we are all dreamers, and we are mystified by our own dreams.

Will science ever tell us anything about the dream story that unfolds itself nightly? What can we possibly learn about the content of dreams—our own, and those of our entire dream-haunted species?

DREAM BANK

It struck Calvin Hall that if enough random dreams could be gathered and studied, a pattern would emerge. So back in the 1940s, this early specialist in dreams became a tireless collector.

It was Hall's own dream that the dream bank would represent a wide range of nighttime reveries. The collection would include the dreams of old, middle-aged, and young people of both sexes and of many backgrounds. Above all, he had broken away from the previous practice of assembling dreams largely from patients undergoing treatment for mental disorders. Hall was seeking what he called "the dreams of normal people."

Many dreams were provided by volunteers in his own sleep laboratories in Miami, Florida and later at Santa Cruz, California. He also sought written dream records from research centers throughout the world. In time, his institute had a stock of fifty thousand dreams.

The data poured in from widely flung bedchambers. One study that was fed into Hall's computers compared seven thousand dreams of students—half of them Japanese, the other half American. Also in Hall's collection were the night visions of Peruvian mountaineers, Nigerian tribesmen, Irish fisher folk, Eskimo seal hunters. Dream details pictured the native habitats and customs of various cultural groups, and yet these diverse accounts contained many common themes as well—among them birth and death, quest and discovery, triumph and defeat. Dreams of traveling, facing danger, finding treasure, floating in space, struggling with foes, suffering frustration were also common, as were dreams of being pursued, lost, saved, loved, and despised.

To classify this vast collection, Hall categorized the dreams according to content. Who were the people taking part in the dream story and what were they doing? What objects appeared and in what setting? What were the events that occurred in the dream? Did it have a happy ending or a sad one?

Analysis of the subject matter of the collected dreams revealed a few surprises. People do not ordinarily dream about the news of the day, foreign affairs, prominent people, the outcome of elections. Nor do they commonly dream about their jobs, their studies, their household chores, church, or community activities. Instead, dreams are much more personal.

The dreamer may be central and active in the "plot," or he may simply be a spectator or bystander. And while the "cast of characters" often includes friends or members of the dreamer's own family, Hall discovered that four out of every ten characters in dreams are strangers to the dreamer. Others may be people seen or met casually in the dim past.

What goes on in the dream? The dreamer is often in the midst of some kind of movement or local travel—riding, walking, running, jumping, climbing. A great many dreams are quiet, with the characters talking, sitting, or watching. Less often, the dreamer is engaged in strenuous activity. These are samples:

"I dreamed I was a shepherd tending a flock of big ladybugs."

"I was driving into a busy intersection, but the brakes of the car wouldn't work."

"I put a nickel in the slot machine and out poured a jackpot of dirty dishes."

"Some other guys and me were robbing a big super-market, but we got caught because we had to wait in line to get out."

Often dreams are quite dull. But the dreaming mind is a storyteller, and the "plots" may be simple or complex, drawn-out or brief, factual or fantastic. And though many dreams are too trivial to recount, others are rich in action, humor, color, and excitement. This is the type we usually hear about when someone sits down to breakfast saying, "Listen, I just had the craziest dream. . . ."

STORY TIME

Dreams begin in the middle. We find ourselves involved in a situation, a conflict, a crisis.

"I turned on this big fireman's hose, but I can't shut it off."

"I am kissing my cousin whom I don't really like."

"I can't find my way out of a dark cave full of bats with flashing eyes."

"I am flying over the city in a beautiful glider when I know I should be down below minding my baby sister."

Sometimes the setting itself is an important part of the dream. We are at a school picnic or a stock car race. We are in a Persian mosque, a funeral home, or a scene straight out of a recent TV program or book we've read.

"I am talking to three corpses in the county morgue."

"I was riding a motorcycle backward up the side of a mountain."

"My friend and I are rummaging through a trunk full of old dolls."

"I was swimming in a pool when the water suddenly turned into raspberry Jell-O."

The dreamer is rarely alone. Usually several others are present. And as the happenings develop, surprising attitudes of the dreamer toward the other characters may be revealed.

The dream sometimes draws on events long-forgotten. But often it is based on something that happened the day before—even though the dream version may be so scrambled that the events are hardly recognizable. People may appear with others they don't even know, and often they do and say the strangest things.

Our dreams sometimes come in series. At least, there are objects, persons, or events in them that may reappear. Sometimes these chains occur in the dreams of one night. Or a person's dreams over a period of time may be linked together by common themes, patterns, or moods.

"Sweet dreams!" is a common good-night wish. But many dreams are not sweet, pleasant, or even middling. Some are quite disturbing.

That finding came out of a survey of more than a thousand dreams of young men and women college students. For every dream with happy happenings, seven were full of woe. In the analysis of these dreams, only one-fourth were at all enjoyable. Two out of five were fearsome. The dreamers often awoke from a sense of having been chased by human enemies, beasts, or monsters, and usually they lost the race.

In our sleeping adventures, we are often lost, hunted, or searching for someone or something. There is a frustrating sense of not being able to make oneself heard or of trying to remember some lost but important fact. We find ourselves in some terrible moral conflict involving good and evil, or else we seek pleasure while enduring pain.

Unfortunately, the problem in the dream usually remains unsolved. Things do not often wind their way to a neat conclusion as they do in storybooks. We may be awakened just as it seems that matters are about to be settled. However, even one more hour of sleep may not allow us to complete a romantic episode, or save us from goblins, the death sentence, or a losing battle.

According to one well-known theory, all dreaming is a kind of wishful thinking. Supposedly, the visions of the night fulfill the frustrations of the day. A popular romantic song of years ago expressed the idea this way: "A dream is a wish your heart makes. . . ."

If only that were true! We then might enjoy our sleeping reveries more. Unfortunately, our chances of having pleasant dreams are slim. Often sleep churns up episodes we will dread when awake, or people we really like appear in the worst of guises. Sometimes we see ourselves in a terrible light.

Thus, more often than not, we awake anxious and troubled. Sometimes our sleep has been restless—the bed-clothes are rumpled, and we arise in a trembling fright. At such times we are grateful for the ringing alarm clock, and thankful that it was "only a dream!"

NIGHT WALKERS AND MARES

Bedtime is a varied adventure. Instead of plunging at once into the depths of slumber, we doze on our pillows, nodding our way gently into the soft fog of oblivion. More often than we may realize, we dream in color. All our senses are alert. We are not only seeing images and hearing voices, but we are touching, tasting, and smelling as well.

It is before and after dreaming that the sleeper's physical

Anxiety by Edvard Munch, Collection, The Museum of Modern Art, New York, Abby Aldrich Rockefeller Fund

O, I have passed a miserable night,
So full of ugly sights, of ghastly dreams.

—William Shakespeare, *Richard III* I.iv.

movements reach their nightly peaks. In the Stanford University Sleep Disorders Clinic and Laboratories, William C. Dement explains: "Dreaming involves an awake brain in a paralyzed body." And only as the sleeping mind becomes less active and dreaming subsides do the muscles become free to function. It is during this non-REM phase that sleepers are more likely to snore, wet their beds, yawn and stretch, or walk about.

No phase of sleep is more veiled in fables than is sleepwalking. How much of the folklore is true? A recent study was made with a group of habitual sleepwalkers.

Contrary to what most people believe, research revealed that this activity does not usually take place during periods of intense dreaming. Only rarely are the walkers acting out a dream. No matter how long or adventuresome the walk, the sleeper generally awakes with no recollection of ever having left the bed. Electronic monitors may confirm that the minds of the walkers are not ordinarily in an active dreaming phase.

Throughout one experiment, special equipment was used in order to give the walkers plenty of leeway. As they wandered, they trailed after them long braids of wires that kept them hooked up to the EEG recording their brain waves.

What made the scene even more eerie were the blank, staring eyes of the sleepers. They seemed fairly capable of finding their way around furniture and through doorways, and yet they gave no sign of observing or recognizing the researchers as they passed.

However, there is no guardian angel that keeps sleepwalkers from harm. Numerous records tell of sleepwalkers being injured and even killed during their strolls.

Research shows that both bed-wetting and sleepwalking recur in successive generations of some families. Bed-wetting is common among small children, particularly boys, and they seem to outgrow this trait when they get into their teens.

Among the strangest experiences of the night is the so-called lucid dream. Asleep and dreaming, we are sometimes aware that we *are* dreaming! We may even ask ourselves, "Is this a dream?" and then answer, "Yes, it is."

Among the most disturbing kinds of dreams are the recurrent ones. Some return periodically throughout our lives. Often they are unpleasant, or even threatening. A single haunting scene is replayed from time to time in almost identical fashion. The familiar story moves toward the same agonizing climax, and the dreamer is powerless to stop the show. Here is the way some have appeared:

"Fierce iguanas chase me, but my legs are like spaghetti."

"I am a small boy in a large public library, surrounded by a gang of young hoodlums, all grinning in a terrible way."

"I am being swept away by floodwaters, trying desperately to hold onto my father's arm."

"I am standing near a blazing building, not knowing for sure—did I cause the fire or not?"

Nightmares are of two breeds. The first kind is actually a sudden awakening from dreamless sleep. The sleeper is aroused with a terrifying sense of being crushed, choked, drowned, or smothered. Or there may be a feeling of falling to one's death, or of being unable to move.

In this so-called night terror, small children often scream out in the late evening. Gagging and coughing, wild-eyed and hysterical, they are hardly able to sob out an explanation of what happened. Sometimes they will cry pitifully for a long while, needing comfort and reassurance.

What is the cause of night terror? Disconnected from any dream, this disturbance, felt as a pain, spasm, or seizure, is believed to be triggered by some upset in the body that shocks the sleeper wide awake.

Night terror is different from the thoroughbred nightmare—a lurid dream that usually comes just before morning. In olden times, it was whispered that nightmares were caused by poisonous vapors drifting about through the hours of darkness, or by sleeping on your back, or by eating cucumbers. And supposedly they occurred only during certain phases of the moon. Still another myth held that nightmares were the result of such unwise bedtime eating habits as mixing pickled peppers with minced pie and cold beans.

But a nightmare is more than a bellyache. It is a vivid dream—horribly real—in which the dreamer may be tortured, pursued, attacked, or killed in an imaginative variety of ways. The nightmare has a highly emotional quality. The victim is full of fear, anxiety, frustration, or rage. Typically, the dreamer is being unfairly treated, unable to flee or fight back, tricked, betrayed, trapped, outnumbered. The nightmare is high drama with the dreamer as the tragic hero or heroine.

What does all this chaotic dreaming mean? Is it the mere mischievous playacting of the idle mind, devoid of reason or rules? That ancient query still stands. As yet, we have no single accepted answer to clearly explain our night visions. Instead, we have a thousand theories—some as fantastic as our most fanciful dreams.

Seekers of Meaning 6

Of what do geese dream? They dream of corn!

—Sigmund Freud,
Interpretation of Dreams

Among the ruins of an Egyptian city on the Nile Delta, one can still see a hut with this sign over the door: "I interpret dreams, having the god's mandate to do so."

Early dream interpreters worked their trade alongside spell casters, faith healers, fortune-tellers, charm sellers. Some dream interpreters sold their services to the general public, but many vied for the special favors of monarchs.

From the fading records of ancient kingdoms, one can learn of the perilous careers of professional dream-tellers. Some who guessed wrong lost their heads. Others mastered the art of finding within a puzzling royal dream some favorable prophecy or piece of good advice. Should the prediction happen to prove true, the dream seer could expect to live in luxury—at least until the next test of his powers.

The interpretation of dreams is still not the most secure of occupations. However, today's practitioners usually rely on a theory of some kind—a set of guidelines. They may follow the principles of some established school or faith or system.

Of course, there are others who question whether dreams

have any meaning at all. The doubt is voiced by some experts in the field who say that in dreaming, the mind is at work, but only at a very low level. They compare the dreamer's brain to a high-powered engine that is idling.

Holders of this opinion argue that dreaming is merely simple, limited thought. They say that the higher centers of the brain—those capable of involved reasoning, finely tuned to abstract ideas, directed by free will and able to solve complex problems—are unused in dreaming. Instead, they believe that the dream is told in primitive and childlike picture stories. The dreaming mind, they add, is dominated by emotions instead of reason, swayed by fancies and fears, confused as to what is real and unreal, and completely out of the dreamer's control.

However, most of those who study dreams take the opposite view. They believe that dreams are not merely series of random images, but that they actually have something to say to us. It is rather widely agreed that dreams do contain information on some aspects of the dreamer's life or personality.

There are many other disagreements between the experts. Some say dreams contain messages that come from somewhere outside the person. The more popular view is that the dreamer alone is the source of the dream and everything in it.

"Master your dreams!" is the advice given by those who suggest there are ways to control your mind during sleep and fill your dreaming hours with useful or pleasant experiences. The contrary opinion is that it is unwise to tamper with your dreams. By changing the content of the dream, it is said, one loses the opportunity to learn the important messages contained in it.

For many psychologists, dreams offer insights into personality. Some use dreams as clues to a person's state of mind. They pay close attention to the dream account, just as other doctors may listen to a patient's report of a pain, a fever, or a dizzy spell. Such an approach examines dreams for clues to mental disorders and their possible cures.

Others see dreams as having much wider significance. This view holds that all of us can benefit by studying our own dreams. The dream, it is said, is one of many paths toward deeper self-understanding. It may be used as a guide to enlarging and enriching our lives.

It is not easy for us to thread our way through the bewildering maze of dream theories. And yet, it is probably important to examine every idea and to listen to every voice:

"A dream is a letter to oneself."

"Every dream is a confession."

"We are poets in our dreams."

"Dreams are hopes that can be realized."

"In the dream we can do things we would never dream of doing!"

"The dream clears the garbage from our minds and makes room for new information."

"A dream is a fantasy of the future that prepares us for real life."

"Our dreams link us with the dreams of the rest of humankind."

"The dream is our own reward or punishment for the way we live."

The Labyrinth by Robert Vickrey, Collection of the Whitney Museum of American Art, New York

Our life is two-fold: Sleep hath its own world,
A boundary between the things misnamed
Death and existence: Sleep hath its own world,
And a wide realm of wild reality.

—Lord Byron, *The Dream*

"Dreams are the 'music' of ten untrained fingers drifting idly over piano keys."

Seek and you can probably find any dream theory you could want—or you may even dream up one of your own. Many dream interpreters openly admit that they are groping in the dark. Others claim that they hold the lamp of everlasting truth.

DREAM MAKING

Old and stubborn beliefs still insist that the dreaming mind can glimpse the secrets of the darkest past, foresee the future, perceive events at some distant place, soar beyond the barriers of life and death.

Does the dream so greatly enlarge our ordinary powers? Countless stories tell of the strange delivery of messages through the medium of dreams.

An Austrian bishop dreamed one night that he received a letter which read: "My wife and I have been victims of a political crime at Sarajevo." The signature that appeared on this odd message was that of Archduke Franz Ferdinand, who years earlier had been a pupil of this same bishop.

On June 28, 1914, ten hours after the churchman had awakened from this frightening dream, the archduke and his wife were, in fact, murdered at Sarajevo. This was the assassination that touched off World War I.

In the year 1966, a child who lived in a Welsh mining community reported having a nightmare in which she saw the town being buried in a landslide. She, along with a hundred others, died soon afterward in just such a disaster.

In another case, a mother heard in her sleep the dying outcry of her son who was then in a distant part of the world. Soon, a letter came from him, delayed en route, in which he said he had fallen ill. After some days, the mother received a report of her son's death. He had died on the same night of the mother's dream.

Such perplexing tales only add to the number of beliefs still held today on the nature of dreams and dreamers. Many people cling steadfastly to the idea that it is solely the dreamer who makes the dream. No, others argue, the dream is a means of receiving and sending communications.

The dream vision, some believe, is the work of supernatural forces. Supposedly, certain people are gifted with almost magical powers of dream perception. It is said that so-called psychic persons have the power to flash messages into the minds of dreamers remote in space and even in time.

Dream telepathy—the sending of messages to a person asleep—is now the subject of much scientific study. The Maimonides Community Mental Health Center in Brooklyn, New York, is one of several laboratories where such research is going on.

The experiments are set up in such a way as to avoid either the accidental or deliberate tampering with the test results. Thought messages are "beamed" through three closed doors over a distance of one hundred feet to a sleeping subject. Later, the dreamer's visions are reported and compared with the messages.

The sponsors of this research, many of them noted scientists, say there is much evidence of telepathy. Other observers of the experiments are less impressed with the results. Meanwhile, the research continues.

Some consider hypnosis to be a valuable aid in understanding dreams. This is a mental state in which a person responds readily to the suggestions of the hypnotist. The hypnotic trance outwardly resembles sleep but has few of sleep's characteristics.

In a typical experiment, a hypnotized person is instructed as to what is to be included in a later dream. The subject is then released completely from the hypnotic state and a while later retires for sleep. Does this sleeper then carry out the dream instructions given during hypnosis? It is claimed that such experiments show a high success rate. A significant portion of the content of such posthypnotic dreams contains material suggested by the hypnotist.

While many researchers go ahead to advance our knowledge about dreams, there are also some who have turned backward for answers. They are busy sifting through the old dream lore of religious cults, reviving the mystical practices of primitive societies, and in some cases, fashioning modern fads out of ancient rituals.

One group follows the teachings of a small Yoga sect native to the towering plateaus of Tibet. These self-styled "masters of the dream" practice a strict and constant program of meditation, breathing and body exercises, and self-induced trances. We are told that, as a result, the devotee of this faith is able to hang suspended in a state somewhere between sleeping and waking. It is said that these Yogis are able to study, analyze, and control their own dreams while they are going on.

Control of one's own brain waves is also being advocated by those who experiment with biofeedback. The sponsors of this method say that we can train ourselves, through the use of certain electronic instruments, to exert power over the workings of the nervous system both while we are awake and asleep.

Control of behavior, including dream behavior, is the goal of one major trend in modern psychology. One of this group's principal methods is to offer rewards for desired behavioral changes. Total power over our dreaming is suggested by another group who say that we can turn all our bad dreams into good ones.

Some of these dream changers have traveled as far as the high jungles of Malaysia to seek support for their theory. Here they found the Senoi, primitive folk far removed from the mainstream of today's world. In each household of this tribe, the day begins with the family's retelling of the night's dreams. The children are encouraged to report how they behaved during their dreams. In encountering enemies, wild animals, or evil spirits, did they act fearful and timid? If so, they are scolded and punished. But if they faced up bravely to any danger in their dreams—if they attacked their attackers —they are praised and rewarded.

In this fashion, the Senoi train their children and themselves to enter actively into their dreams—to grapple with villains, defeat the demons, and chase out all foes. What's more, they demand that their enemies pay a price for their mischief!

Supposedly, the Senoi sleep peacefully, their nights free of fear.

THE CODE OF SYMBOLS

Dreams inform, comfort, advise, warn, punish, heal. . . . For those who believe they are useful at all, there seems to be no end to their uses. And it is widely believed that they achieve this usefulness through the language of symbols. In fact, symbols and the translation of them are important parts of dream interpretation.

Early in our lives, we begin to think in symbols. A flag stands for nationhood. A skull means death. A crown, a lion, a bell—all are symbols for certain ideas.

For many of us, the appearance of certain images in dreams quickly conveys meanings. We may be stopped by a roadblock, see the rising sun, or get carried away in a torrent. We may climb a ladder, or have a burden to carry, or find ourselves lost in the woods. Such dream symbols may tell us something about ourselves.

One dream theory states that the whole dream is a symbol, as is everything and everyone in it. According to this theory, all dream images represent ourselves so that the awakened dreamer may ask, "If all elements of the dream are myself, what would these various parts say if they were to speak?" In this fashion, the dream can be reviewed and relived. The dreamer speaks. So do all other dream elements—strangers, companions, animals, objects. With the dreamer acting some or all of the parts, the full moon of one dream may speak out, as may the surrounding hills that witnessed the dream events. The lake has its say, as does the sailboat on which the dream plot unfolded. After one or all of these roles have been played out, the meaning of the dream may be clarified.

Many dream interpreters have developed great skill in translating symbols, finding hidden meanings in words or phrases, relating dream images to events in the dreamer's waking life. For example, the dreamer was at the side of a swimming pool but she feared to take the plunge into the water. Does that perhaps express her own uncertainty about her impending marriage?

One young fellow dreamed he was trapped by a flood of some chalky white liquid that was rising higher and higher, threatening to drown him. What was that fluid? Awake, the dreamer recognized it as the milk shake he wanted to buy on the previous day. And too many milk shakes were making him fat!

In another case, a dreamer found himself surrounded by a band of outlaws. Later, he is aware that these were his wife's relatives—his demanding "in-laws."

The dream symbol may disguise something or someone from our waking lives. Our parents may appear as Adam and Eve. A much loved friend may take on the form of a priceless jewel. If we are "at sea" about some problem, we may dream we are thrashing about in the ocean. And if someone has "put us down," we may dream of ourselves in just such a symbolic position.

What accounts for the strange assortment of people who appear in our dreams? "The dreamer is the author of his dream and determines who should be invited into it" is the opinion of Calvin S. Hall. It is his view that these are usually people about whom the dreamer has "mixed feelings of affection and antagonism," emotions that are still unresolved.

Like other modern dream theorists, Hall stresses the idea that the dreamer's "deep-down" feelings during waking hours are later reflected in dreams. In his opinion, a "bad dream" may occur when the dreamer has gratified a forbidden wish.

Visions of the night, we are told, may reveal what the dreamer was unable or unwilling to confront during wakefulness. These buried sentiments may include the disturbing experiences of the preceding days, unpleasant childhood memories, doubts about the future, fears of other persons, concerns about shortcomings and weaknesses. Instead of being expressed openly, these painful thoughts are hidden behind puzzling images, secret symbols. And the people of dreams may appear in many disguises.

It was and is believed by many that dreams could only be properly interpreted under the guidance of an expert. Dreams may be brought to a therapist or analyst. The dreamer might supply some additional related information, but the analyst ordinarily plays the dominant role in determining dream meanings.

We are now being told by some, however, that we ourselves may study and learn what the dream is saying. This modern concept is that most of us are perfectly capable of understanding our own dreams. We are not necessarily dependent on professional help or on years of costly private sessions with an analyst.

The well-known image of the analyst is represented by Sigmund Freud. This famous doctor developed a system of treating his mental patients which he called psychoanalysis—a method still widely used. At the core of Freud's therapy was the interpretation of dreams.

Almost a century ago, he began his career in Vienna, Austria in utter poverty and failure. Throughout his early years, he was debt-ridden, his ambitions frustrated, his ideas ignored. He was then an unknown neurologist, struggling to make a living for himself and his family. In the final years of the last century, Freud began to recognize how deeply the sufferings of his patients were reflected in their night visions.

"What a pity one cannot live from interpreting dreams," Freud wrote to a friend in 1897. He was then at work on a book, *The Interpretation of Dreams*. Unfortunately, his own research was rather sparse. The dreams he studied were his own and those of his friends and patients. The latter were people afflicted with a variety of nervous disorders—anxieties, obsessions, delusions, hysteria, madness. They brought to Freud vivid accounts of those dreams they thought would be most useful in relieving their suffering.

Freud did not limit his book to describing his treatment methods. Instead, he offered a general explanation of the dreams of all humankind.

His book made hardly a stir. "I am not finding it easy to wrest attention from the world," he complained, "for it is thick-skinned and hard of hearing." It took him most of his lifetime to make himself heard.

Until his death, Freud remained a very controversial figure. Yet his work became so well-known that he himself was regarded as the very symbol of the dream.

This one man was to dominate dream theory and dream therapy for half a century. What were these ideas of his that seemed to haunt the world?

THE FREUD YEARS

Sigmund Freud appeared as a latter-day version of the ancient dream interpreter—the oracle of night's dark riddles, the healer who uses sleep visions in order to cure.

However, Freud stripped away ancient superstitions. He built his theory around the concept that the dream is produced entirely by the mind of the dreamer. To Freud all dreams were important and contained significant information. The problem for the analyst, he believed, was to sift out that meaning from the code of mixed symbols in which it was hidden.

Freud was a brilliant, sensitive man with a marvelous talent for putting together the bits and pieces of both the patient's dreaming and waking experiences. His studies convinced him that there was but a single underlying theme to be found in the dreams of all dreamers—the fulfillment of a wish.

He cited the dreams of children as examples. One child cried out in her sleep for strawberries. Another dreamed of a long boat ride—the very trip she had pleaded with her parents for on the previous day. In another example, a boy had been disappointed in not being taken to the top of a mountain. However, he did manage to reach the peak that very night—in a dream.

"The common element in all these children's dreams is obvious," Freud declared. "All of them fulfilled wishes which were active during the day but had remained unfulfilled. The dreams were simple and undisguised *wish fulfillments.*"

This moody genius wrote numerous case histories of mental patients, showing that they had buried within themselves certain shame-filled desires which had twisted their reason and disturbed their waking behavior. Ashamed of their passions and lusts, they expressed them in dreams, said Freud.

This theory, for all its emphasis on the dark side of human nature, proved to be a very powerful doctrine. Outwardly, Freud seemed to be saying, we may all appear as proper citizens—respectable, law-abiding, considerate, and sensible. But there is another person buried within each of us, one with guilty desires, irrational hatreds, driving ambitions, unanswered needs.

Supposedly, this secret part of us is a demon that dares not show itself openly, even to ourselves. Instead, it appears in our night visions, concealed in a variety of disguises. In the dream, this other self acts out behaviors we repress during our waking hours.

Many have challenged Freud's insistence that all dreams

may be traced to unfulfilled wishes. Other ideas of his about dreams are also disputed, particularly his notion that the dream acts as "the guardian of sleep" by quieting one's troublesome desires. It was pointed out to him that a great many dreams disturb rather than safeguard sleep.

Many of his most devoted students and followers disagreed with his concepts. Some later developed their own dream theories and systems of treatment.

Probably the most famous of these was Carl Gustav Jung, a Swiss doctor who came to rival Freud as an authority on the meaning of dreams. For Jung, who died in 1961, the dream was "a self-portrait." He disagreed with Freud that dreams fulfill wishes, and he objected to Freud's stress on the sexual meanings of dreams.

The dream, as Jung saw it, represented realities of the dreamer's life. In his view, the dream, properly interpreted, was "a genuine expression of the inner life," with all its conflicts and its potentialities.

It is said by many authorities on dreams that we are now living in the "post-Freudian era"—not merely because Sigmund Freud has been dead since 1939, but because some of his theories have been shaken by breakthroughs in today's scientific study of dreams.

For example, Freud believed that most of the sleeper's night is passed in dreamlessness—the mind lost in "unconscious processes." According to him, it was only at the end of that long, dark period that the dream suddenly flared into the sleeper's vision. In Freud's view, the dream "is like a firework which takes hours to prepare but goes off in a moment." Years of laboratory testing has now proved that some form of dreamlike activity goes on throughout sleep, with many a full-fledged, storylike dream.

Unfortunately, Freud lived in a time when dreams had not yet come under scientific investigation. He knew nothing of the inner physiological changes that accompany sleep and dreaming. Nor did he have the advantage of today's systematic examination of huge numbers of dreams. From this modern data, we have a very different idea about the process and content of dreaming.

During his long career, Freud grappled with the question of why dreams occur, and in his wish fulfillment theory, he thought he had found the perfect answer. But the whys behind dreaming still stand, and today's scientists continue to search for the answers.

Those who probe for the function of dreams ask another question: Do we dream in order to sleep—or do we sleep in order to dream?

A Matter of Survival   7

*I have called this principle, by which each
slight variation, if useful, is preserved, by
the term Natural Selection.*

—Charles Darwin, *The Origin of Species*

Do we need our dreams? The very question seems to point
a way toward the answer. Let's see how well we do without
them.

In 1959, such reasoning led William Dement on a series
of REM deprivation experiments. REM scribbles on the
EEG, triggered by the brain of the sleeping volunteer,
signaled Dement into action. The dreamer was quickly
roused from his reveries. These awakenings were repeated
throughout the night—every time the telltale REM waves
reappeared. The REM-time arousals were continued the
following night, and on the night after.

Dement soon found himself in trouble. The more he
stopped REM periods, the faster they recurred! "By the third
night," Dement later recalled, "I was trotting in and out of
the subjects' bedrooms so fast that I could barely keep it up."

Unaware of it themselves, the volunteers in these experiments carried on a fierce struggle for REM sleep. After a
dreamless night or two, they went into dreaming the minute
they dozed off! REM crowded out the other stages of sleep.

The experimenters found it increasingly difficult to keep

REM out of the EEG record. After five nights, the normal four or five REM periods per night reached as high as thirty-six!

Exhausted, Dement was just about ready to give up. It had become almost impossible to awaken his subjects in order to interrupt their dream periods. Through vigorous struggles, the volunteers had to be wrestled awake and hoisted upright. By shouting in their ears, the eye movements could be halted—but only temporarily.

Said Dement, "The only way dreaming could be stopped was to drag the subject out of bed, walk him around until he was awake, and then keep him awake."

These frantic experiences were convincing demonstrations of an inner desperate drive for REM sleep. However, what happened on the following nights was even more dramatic. Each REM-starved volunteer, now permitted to sleep peacefully in the lab, proceeded to make up for the lost REM time!

Almost from the moment heads hit pillows, the REM patterns began to appear on the EEG. What followed throughout this first "recovery" night were astonishingly long dream periods. The total night's dream time was four times greater than usual. Some REM periods went on for three hours. On succeeding nights, this make-up pattern continued.

Clearly, Dement's volunteers could not tolerate the shortening of their dream time. Some urge from within compelled them to catch up whatever they had lost. But what was being lost? Does the mind cry out for the storylike visions of sleep? Or does the physical being actually require that complex package of activities known as the REM state?

One view is that the human mind periodically tends to wander off into free thought. These flights of imagination are dreams during sleep, and daydreams during wakefulness. Some experimental evidence shows that when a sleeper is deprived of dreams, fantasy thoughts increase in the waking state. As we have also seen, some research has linked our wakeful behavior to the ninety-minute dream cycle.

Recently, a group of students grappled with the ninety-minute REM cycle in a novel way. These were freshmen at Stanford University, members of Dement's class on sleep and dreams. Joy Kelley, an eighteen-year-old, was the first volunteer for a six-day test. She agreed to live by a schedule of thirty minutes asleep and sixty minutes awake, continuously throughout the days and nights.

The students were testing one of the theories about REM—that its function is to break up the long night every ninety minutes with some needed mental activity. If this were true, then perhaps REM sleep could be eliminated through one-hour intervals of wakefulness. At least such a result seemed possible.

Joy Kelley had little trouble with a round-the-clock schedule of a thirty-minute "night" followed by a sixty-minute "day." She did succeed in sleeping during all but one of her ninety-one "nights." And this healthy young woman showed no ill effects from the experiment. However, neither she nor the five other students who followed her schedule succeeded in substituting awake time for REM sleep. Throughout their short sleeps, REM periods were recorded with regularity.

REM deprivation experiments have been carried on in

Silence by Odilon Redon, Collection, The Museum of Modern Art, New York, Lillie P. Bliss Collection

Come, blessed barrier between day and day.

—William Wordsworth, *To Sleep*

many ways. Some have used a variety of drugs—many of which have been shown to limit REM sleep. And instead of featuring human subjects, much of the research has turned to the cat. This animal is among the greatest of sleepers and is well known for its catnaps.

The laboratory in Lyon, France devised a practical way of depriving cats of their REM periods, basing the experiment on the natural dislike of cats for the feel of water on their bodies. In this experiment, the cat is seated on a small stone island in the midst of a large pool of water. The cat sits like a sphinx on its perch throughout the early stages of sleep. But at the onset of REM, neck muscles naturally go limp. The cat's head droops, its nose hits the water. Quickly it wakes, and the REM state has been stopped.

The REM-deprived subject, human or animal, shows temporary signs of strain, anxiety, discomfort. But the ordeal has not resulted in any permanent damage or mental disorder. Human subjects have lost REM sleep continuously for sixteen days, and cats for seventy. Eventually they recovered. Dement has concluded from his research that "the REM state does not appear to be absolutely necessary to maintain life in the adult animal." And yet, a stubborn question remains. What is the biological significance of REM?

A MAMMAL TRAIT

I tape recorded a conversation with a biologist friend who said, "The dream, that's still the riddle. We keep asking ourselves, 'What is the use of it?'"

"Does it have to have a use?"

"Living species do not ordinarily continue to hand down traits that are useless. Every inborn feature is tested throughout countless generations as to whether it helps or hinders in the struggle for survival."

"Does that mean that we know how every trait of every animal evolved?"

"Certainly not. But it does boggle the mind even to think about the survival value of dreams!"

The survival value of dreams . . . We may be able to think up a thousand human uses for dreams, but none of them may reveal an underlying biological necessity for dreaming. The dream is not a human invention. And its basic function may only be explained by going back to where dreamlike behavior first appeared in the evolution of species.

Who was that first dreamer? Was it perhaps a distant ancestor of the fringe-toed lizard? Some will trace REM sleep back earlier—back to the fish. Others will argue that the dream was originated more recently by the mammals, only two hundred million years ago. The most cautious scientists will not admit that any but human beings dream.

In any case, REM sleep is a trait of mammals. The one possible exception is the spiny anteater. From this sleepy, egg-laying, burrowing mammal, researchers have not been able to coax a single REM—and they have lost a good deal of sleep over it. But REMs do appear in mammals as primitive as opossums and as complex as human beings. This trait, along with hair, warm blood, and glands that produce mothers' milk, is one mammals have in common.

In addition to physical features, mammals have inherited

many behavior patterns—inborn tendencies to act in certain ways. Dreams or REMs are one kind of behavior—and what a peculiar behavior it is!

Dreaming is involuntary—beyond the will or control of the organism. But although the behavior is inborn and unlearned, the content of the dream is not. It is made up of material taken from life experiences.

An inherited behavior can ordinarily be matched to the particular environment in which the species lives. However, REM sleep is universal among mammals. In fact, few types of behavior are so common to so many animals—though the duration of REM sleep varies for individuals and species.

Some of the most necessary behaviors of living things, timed to the ceaseless biological clocks of nature, occur rhythmically. REM sleep is one such behavior. An animal may miss a meal or skip some other event that is part of its life-style. But any loss of REM sleep must be made up immediately. In REM deprivation experiments with both human and animal subjects, this recovery drive has appeared consistently.

Some behavior patterns are seasonal. Others change with the shifting conditions of life. Not so with dreamlike behavior. It remains a consistent phenomenon, regardless of the environment. Many innate behaviors appear at only one stage in the life cycle, but REM sleep continues throughout the lifetime of the mammal as a daily or nightly event.

Ordinarily it is not difficult to understand how an inborn behavior helps to sustain life. The common animal behaviors connected with feeding, home making, mobility, fighting, escape, pairing, and mating are readily seen for their survival value. But the lifetime advantage of dreaming eludes us. We are unable to explain the dream as a life-and-death need.

Those who search for the mechanism of dreaming tell us that it is located in the "oldest" part of the brain. They say that the structures and chemistry of REM stem from that simpler part of the human brain which is similar to the brains found in lower animals. This primitive, lower brain was present in species that existed long before human beings with their so-called higher brain centers.

It is clear that the dream is something inherited from the remote past. In fact, it was so vital to survival that it persisted in all mammalian species. They consistently handed down this trait throughout the millions of generations during which the mammals developed, spread, and grew to dominate the world. The dreamers flourished.

THE MISSING PLUS

"If sleep does not serve an absolutely vital function, then it is the biggest mistake the evolutionary process has ever made."

Allan Rechtschaffen does not believe such a "mistake" was made. But this is his wry way of confessing that he has not discovered the unknown function of sleep and dreams—nor have any of his colleagues. My mission in seeing him was to learn the latest exploits of a man who has constantly been in the forefront in this field. This also gave me a chance to visit the University of Chicago site where the new era in sleep-dream research had its beginnings in 1952.

Rechtschaffen and his cramped but productive laboratory occupy the top floor of a recycled apartment building just off campus. It was here that we mulled the "function" problem.

While admitting to his own frustration, Rechtschaffen is by no means discouraged. The theories about function are numerous. Many do not stand up well under close examination. Most have not yet been thoroughly researched. Some are promising.

Still in early experimental work are the theories of function that link dreaming with certain essential physiological changes in the body. Some scientists believe that a brain chemical called serotonin is "the crucial substance that turns dreams on and off." One laboratory has developed the hypothesis that during dreaming, the brain rebuilds its supplies of certain chemicals that are used up during the day. A psychological theory of dream function states that REM sleep sorts and stores the information that has come in during the day. Another view is that during REM sleep the dreamer explores solutions to wakeful problems. A fourth idea is that dreams act as emotional outlets.

It is argued that some of these suggested functions may be significant in terms of the human mind and human needs, but they are not so easy to apply to animals. Perhaps we just do not yet know enough about a sloth's thinking processes, or a shrew's feelings.

A good deal of theorizing has centered around the research into the "best" and "worst" dreamers in the animal world, for the contrast is sharp between cat and mouse, predator and prey. Of the cat's lengthy slumber, fully twenty-nine percent is devoted to the REM state. The mouse has comparatively little time for dreams. Its REM time is less than ten percent of its total sleep.

The same pattern is clear throughout the animal world. Hunting species and meat eaters devote a lot of their sleeping time to the dreamlike state, while the vegetation-eating animals and the hunted have less REM sleep. The exceptions to this pattern are the burrowers, the swimmers, the tree inhabitants, and the night prowlers—that is, the species that are relatively well protected during sleep. They manage to get in more dream time than do other prey species.

Thinking about safety and sleep, some researchers developed the idea that REM may have the function of keeping a sleeping animal alert to danger. According to this theory, the vigorous mental activity of REM sleep may better prepare an animal to deal with an attack. It is said that the REM state begins the process of arousal and even awakens the animal periodically so that it can check its surroundings for possible trouble.

Other researchers see little evidence in support of this theory. In fact, some take an opposite view. They see the dream state as a dangerous one for the animal in the wilderness. Far from being prepared for defense or attack or flight, the dreaming animal is in an almost paralyzed condition. During REM, the large muscles of the body are completely relaxed and unusable, for the very same REM process that turns the brain on "High" reduces muscle tone to "Low."

Rechtschaffen points out that sleeping and dreaming have many obvious disadvantages for the animal in the wild state. During such dormant periods, they are not seeking food, mating, safeguarding either themselves or their off-spring. "With all these *minus* factors," he says, "there must be a big *plus* somewhere!"

Not only are researchers probing the function of dreams, they are also asking the same questions about the uses of REM and sleep. In explaining sleep, Rechtschaffen says that the researcher cannot be content merely with the idea that slumber provides rest, repair, and restoration of the body. "We need to know what it is that is getting restored," he says.

Although dreams and REMs seem closely linked to-gether, they may have distinct functions. As we have seen, REM deprivation experiments have shown an insistent drive in both humans and animals for REM sleep. But even though there is not yet any proof of a comparable need for dream images, such a biological necessity may exist.

A scientist named Howard Roffwarg is given main credit for developing what Rechtschaffen calls "the most viable theory as to why evolution dreamed up the REM period." Roffwarg's studies focus on processes going on in the develop-ing brains of newborns and those about to be born. These early days of life appear to be the most vital time for REM sleep.

Strangely, REM research now turns back to the new-born—where it began!

A USE FOR REM?

To Michel Jouvet, the dream is a paradox—a word that means "not what you might expect." Fittingly, his laboratory in Lyon, France is full of surprises. I found it to be a showcase of novel methods in getting at the whys of dreaming.

Most unusual of all are his experiments with embryos—animals as yet unborn. One of his EEG machines is hooked up to a basketful of eggs. Tiny electrodes, attached to the brains of the unhatched chicks, monitor their sleep. Among his prime subjects are several pink and tender-skinned guinea pigs who were prematurely born. In these developing animals, the lab is studying the REM state or, as Jouvet calls it, "paradoxical sleep."

Jouvet's work follows out a hunch that has hovered about the sleep-dream scientific community for a dozen years or more. Like sleuths on a hot case, investigators have pondered the solution to that number one mystery—the function of dreaming. A series of clues pointed them toward the newborn.

The first hint was the high level of REM sleep in new babies. At birth, their normal daily sleeping time is about eighteen hours. Fully half of that time is spent in dreaming. It is unlikely that these dreams have very much in the way of content—but they are dreams nonetheless.

Undoubtedly it is not only REM sleep that the maturing child needs. Growth hormone, which stimulates the development of bones and regulates other growth processes, is secreted in short bursts and released into the bloodstream. Much of this takes place during slumber, typically during Stage 4 sleep. However, the high REM levels in infant sleep have long been recognized as strong indicators of biological needs.

A baby born prematurely devotes an extraordinary proportion of its sleep time—as much as eighty percent—to REM.

From the time of birth on, the REM rate declines sharply, dropping to about twenty percent where it remains throughout young adulthood and middle age. In old age, REM time shortens even more. And the pattern is the same in animals at various ages.

A second lead toward discovering the function of dreams lay in one of REM's paradoxes—it features a highly active brain in an almost motionless body. As Jouvet puts it, "One may dream that he is running or flying but the body does not move."

The French researcher calls this muscular shutoff "a dangerous mechanism." But it is hazardous only in the sense that the dreaming animal may be exposed to enemies and other risks. However, the highest-level REM periods of life come at a time when the animal is still curled up in the womb or in the protected home environment. In fact, the plentiful REM sleep of the newborn keeps it from wandering about at a time when it is not yet able to cope with peril.

In what way can dreaming possibly be an inherited behavior that is *adaptive*—that better fits the organism for survival? One mark of any inborn feature is that it adapts the organism to its living environment. Some obvious examples are fur, fins, and feathers.

A second test of adaptiveness is whether a trait prepares the organism for the next stage of its life. Some *physical* features which typically serve this need would be the larval form of insects, the eggshell of birds, and the tadpole stage of frogs. And several *behavioral* traits that are adaptive at certain periods in the life of an organism would be the cocoon making of moths, the gaping habits of fledgling birds that prompts feeding, and the clinging of young monkeys to their

mothers swinging swiftly through the trees. These are temporary traits that assist the organism in its further development. And, according to the chief current theory of dream
function, dreaming serves exactly the same purpose. This
view states that the main biological use of REM sleep is
connected with the early formation and maturing of the
nervous system.

Scientists have suggested how mammals may have ac-
quired dreamlike behavior. Mammals appeared on earth as
large-brained creatures—the different species equipped with
intricate sense organs and complex nervous systems that
permitted a wide range of behavior. It is a trait of mammals
that they develop slowly, both in the womb and after birth.
In some species, the young spend long periods of time in the
mother's pouch. Many kinds of mammals begin life dependent, blind, naked. Some of their features are not fully
formed.

Throughout this birth period, the mammal brain is
slowly being readied for its future role. Exercise, excitement,
stimulation—all are necessary for the brain's proper development. Activity is needed in order to build the circuits, con-
nections, and networks of the brain and the rest of the
nervous system.

Where can the developing offspring find such vigorous
stimulation at a time when it is still leading a very sheltered
life? The current theory is that REM sleep provides the
answer. Dreams are a substitute for real life experiences.
REM sleep plunges the developing brain into furious activity.
And the dream pattern begins in the embryo.

According to this view, all mammals evolved in this way,
including our own species. Emerging from the womb with its

inborn traits, the newborn organism crosses over into life in the natural environment. REM sleep provides the bridge, having trained the embryo for the new stage of its life. This seems to researchers a plausible explanation for the dream being part of our biological heritage. Thus it may be that the function of dreams is, as Jouvet sees it, "to program innate behavior."

The French scientist has found support for this view in studying animals *in utero*—before birth. His research seems to show that the rate of REM or paradoxical sleep coincides with the development of the brain. For example, the rat is born with an immature brain and has a very high rate of REM sleep immediately at birth. The guinea pig, born with a more mature brain, has relatively less REM sleep at birth. However, EEG records made of the guinea pig *in utero,* twenty days before birth, show that its total REM sleep is the same as that for the newborn rat.

Jouvet points out that paradoxical sleep may also play a role in the development of learning or memory, or in the maturing of such complicated sensing as the binocular vision of mammals. And while the theory does account for the fact that when deprived of dreams, *adults* suffer no serious effects, Jouvet admits that the theory "does not explain why paradoxical sleep continues into adult life."

The sleep-dream scientists are in hot pursuit of answers. And it is unlikely that they are soon going to run out of questions. I left Lyon with Jouvet's words echoing in my mind: "We shall not be able to explain satisfactorily the functioning of the brain as long as we do not understand why we dream one hundred minutes every night."

Living with Our Dreams   8

In a full lifetime, each of us will perhaps dream a hundred thousand dreams. They are among the most completely personal of our possessions. We own them all. They are ours to share or to keep to ourselves. They are created solely out of materials that we have been collecting all our lives.

Hidden away in the cookie jars of our memory, we have the ingredients of our dreams. These materials fill our treasure chests, ragbags, and private museums of trifles. Like discarded mementos in abandoned attics and picture albums full of images, our half-remembered experiences are stowed away. Like old diaries, they contain fragments of feeling.

Taken together, our dreams are perhaps a portrait of ourselves, a mirror image of the person each of us is.

You may be the kind of dreamer who, like the elephant, never forgets. Or you may be a forgetful one who recalls nothing. Your private dreamworld may be disturbing and fearsome, full of hobgoblins, spooks, and experiences you want to put quickly out of your mind in daylight. On the other hand, you may find your night visions pleasantly curious, will-o'-the-wisps to be endlessly pursued.

Your dreams may either trouble or tranquilize your sleep. Perhaps you are an edgy sleeper, easily roused by a beam of light from a distant star or by the sound of a spider crossing its web. Or else you may be one of those fortunate people who snoozes soundly and dreamfully through storm, crisis, bedlam. Some of us are night owls, late to bed and late to rise. Others are morning larks up with the sun.

Your dreams may be vivid and full of high adventure. Or else they are so dull as to put others to sleep in the re-telling. They are nevertheless your own—unique.

What is their value? Do they merit your close attention? That is something you'll have to decide for yourself. There is no verified information that measures the importance of dreams. As yet, their worth is a matter of belief, opinion, theory.

As we have seen, scientists are probing the evolutionary origins of dreaming and its advantages in survival. However, this line of research may not help us make up our minds about the personal value of dreams. Whatever the biological significance of REM sleep for mammalian species, dreams may have some distinct human uses. Dreams and REMs may serve in ways that are independent from each other. Beyond the matter of species survival, our dreams may contain pro-found meaning for ourselves.

Unfortunately, our dreams do not preserve themselves. From our lifetime bank of a hundred thousand dreams, how many can we save? A small portion of our dreaming—particularly the last dream of each night—may run wildly through our roused minds as we still lie abed. And though some few may be remembered throughout our lives, most of

Tree into Hand and Foot by Pavel Tchelitchew, Collection, The Museum of Modern Art, New York
Mrs. Simon Guggenheim Fund

Some say that gleams of a remoter world
Visit the soul in sleep.

—Percy Bysshe Shelley, *Mont Blanc*

these visions will be forgotten within minutes.

There are some skills to be learned in dream catching and dream keeping. We must remember, however, that our dreams are vagrant butterflies, captured only by those with ready nets.

THE ART OF RECALL

"Friday night's dream on a Saturday told, will always come true, be it never so old." Right or wrong, this children's rhyme does reveal something about the forgetting and remembering of dreams. Very likely, we can recollect a dream if we are not frantically rushing off to school, to work, or to chores. For this reason, Saturday morning may just be the very best time to recall a dream.

It matters little whether we are shaken awake or alarmed out of sleep by a raucous noise. If we are then permitted to linger motionless on dreamland's border, our eyes closed, then it is likely that we still have the dream within our grasp. In that instant, we may be able to reconstruct not only the story, but the faces of people, the events in detail, and many of the feelings we experienced.

There is an old idea that we forget dreams only because we really want to. It is said that we block out of memory those dreams that contain material we are ashamed to recall or are unwilling to face.

More likely, remembrance of dreams relates to the lapse of time between the end of the dream and the beginning of wakefulness. Ordinarily, the dream will begin to fade from memory within ten minutes after the REM period is over. Our most vivid recollections of dreams come when we are awakened in the midst of them, or immediately after they are completed. However, we often awake from a non-REM stage of sleep, long after the dream is finished. There may be a gap of an hour's dreamless time before we are roused from slumber. By then, the vision has probably turned fuzzy. All or part of it has slipped away. Some shadowy after-thoughts might still be there, but as much as we may grope, they are gone—vanished like wind-driven mist.

The easiest dreams to recall are the exciting ones. Whether pleasant or threatening, the remembered dream is the one that has etched itself deep on the mind. It is that intense and strenuous night's happening that may sometimes leave us keyed up and somewhat exhausted. We awake with a dynamic, animated, and radiant vision. The fresh dream may seem unforgettable. But it, too, needs to find a more lasting form if it is to survive.

The advice we get from expert dream collectors is to prepare ourselves the night before. We must carefully plan how we are to trap the dream. Pad and pencil should be placed conveniently at bedside, and the first thoughts, on awakening, should review the entire dream and fix it care-fully in memory. Still drowsy, we must scribble it all down in rapid shorthand. The dream is now our captive!

We can collect a sheaf of such dreams and fill a notebook with them. They become a diary, each event noted and dated. What do we record? Waste no time at the crucial moment in mulling the dream's meaning. That comes later. Instead, set down the occurrence from beginning to end.

Record the time and place, the characters, the setting, everything. Pay special attention to the feelings expressed, the attitudes shown between the dream characters. Were they hostile or friendly? Think about the strangers—or were they known persons in disguise? Leave out no trivial detail, because it may contain a hidden insight. Finally, try to connect the dream with actual events.

The power of dream recall, we are told, is best held by those who treat their dreams as important. These are people who have probably learned from childhood to pay attention to signals from within. In this view, the dream contains valuable information about our personality and behavior. It is an experience that comes through all of our senses. It touches our deepest human emotions and may be understood through the rational power of the brain.

Dreaming is a kind of meditation in complete solitude. The mind is active, but it is free from outside demands. One is alone. All the senses are turned inward. This may be a time to be in touch with intimate feelings, to listen to an inner voice, and, with eyes closed, to "see" one's private self.

SOMETHING TO SHARE

"The dream is a story you were telling yourself while asleep. Can you guess why, or what it was all about?" So speaks Rosalind Cartwright, teacher and director of sleep-dream research at the University of Illinois, Circle Campus. She is a leading scientist in her field, a scientist with an uncommonly human touch.

Cartwright does not agree with those who dismiss this vital portion of our human behavior with the words, "It was only a dream." One focus of her distinguished career centers on the content of dreams. And though she studies them in a scientific setting, she is most interested in what she calls "the human data."

We talked about her own daughters and their growing-up experiences in sharing their dreams. Some mornings, they liked to sort out the pieces of a dream, wondering where each came from and how it might fit into a picture puzzle of meaning.

"The dream is your own product," she recalled telling them, and instead of imposing her own views, she encouraged them toward an understanding of their own dreams.

Cartwright noted that dreams are too often a forbidden topic of conversation. "Dreams do contain intimate and sensitive materials, and they are best discussed by caring people in a kindly and protected atmosphere," she said, adding that the sharing of dreams can be extremely useful.

What can we learn from a dream? Cartwright talked of the ways in which dreams deal with personal problems—the leftovers from ordinary waking experiences. In their dreams, young people often reflect on the difficulties of growing up in a demanding world. In the everyday encounters of life, they are by turns jostled, perplexed, entertained, defeated, gratified, challenged. Often there are fears of "not making it," of being humiliated or overcome by threatening forces mightier than themselves.

Such problems as these, said Cartwright, appear in some form or other in the dreams of young people. The dream will sometimes follow out a nice problem-solving pattern, and the dream story can be traced from the present to similar experiences in the past, then to possible solutions in the future, and finally back to the present. If you've had a "humpty-dumpty day," she said with a warm smile, then the dream may help you put your pieces back together again. You can now face life, feeling, "I am intact!"

She added that dreams, by making use of emotional experiences in a richer way, may afford opportunities for self-exploration not possible during our waking lives. The dream may also reveal rifts between the values and principles we think we believe in and our actual behavior.

Cartwright sees a close link between the dreams of night and the behavior of day. The emotions of one carry over into the other. The person who has not managed to cope well with daytime problems will probably face many of those same problems in the dark of night. "On the other hand," she said with an easy laugh, "go to bed feeling especially good about yourself and you can play in your dreams!"

Her ideas on dreams do not tie Cartwright rigidly to one dogma or another. She doubts whether any single formula or simple theory can possibly explain all of our mental activity of either the day or the night. For each of us, dream life is just as rich and complex as wakefulness, reflecting our many-sided individuality. Cartwright tests her own interpretations of dreams by "goodness of fit." How well do they serve in self-awareness?

Cartwright is dedicated and hardworking, serving as a classroom professor by day and as a research scientist far into the hours of darkness. Her recent experimental work in the sleep lab has centered on how the dream is formed and the relationship between dream images and waking behavior.

She sees the dream mainly as a means for reaching deeper levels of human understanding. But she is firmly committed to experimental and laboratory methods in the quest. Rarely in the past have we used scientific tools to study our own humanness. And for Cartwright, dream research is enormously promising.

Awed by what remains to be done, she is proud of the sound beginnings which she and her colleagues have made thus far. "Groundbreaking," she called it.

THE DREAM LODE

The dream life of our species is like a vast underground vein of precious metal. But all we can see of it is a few outcroppings. Hardly the smallest portion of this submerged lode has been mined. Nor has the mineral been assayed, analyzed, or refined. We are still scratching at the top crust— still at the surface of scientific understanding.

And yet, there have been some important breakthroughs. In a brief span of time, our knowledge of the sleeping mind has deepened. In our pursuit of the dream, we have expanded our familiarity with the brain, the entire nervous system, and the complex biochemistry that triggers inner body functions and outward behavior.

We are discovering unsuspected mental problems through offbeat dream patterns. We are testing the effects of drugs on sleeping animals, finding cures for some who sleep too little or too much, putting people in touch with their own dreams, and giving the medical profession an early warning system for detecting disease through the study of erratic dreaming.

Just a few years ago, we were still tormented by such childhood sleep problems as sleepwalking, bed-wetting, night terrors. Now we can deal with many of these so-called dysomnias, and we also know that young people tend to outgrow them by age twelve or thirteen.

We now understand dreaming for the regular and universal happening that it is. Normal and natural, the dream is the creation of the dreamer's brain—not the plaything of gods, demons, spirits of the restless dead, or creatures of other worlds.

The cycle of dreaming is a life rhythm that was already throbbing when humankind made its first appearance on earth. It remains one of those unseen forces that beats out the tempo of our daily lives.

The scientific work on sleep and dreams has so far been richly rewarding. But who knows whether such success will continue, contract, or expand? Funds from federal and private sources for research are not easily available. Countless other projects clamor for the money. Experimental work—especially the kind that seeks its data directly from human subjects—is costly.

Research grants tend to flow more readily toward projects that bring quick and easy and usable results. Few areas of sleep-dream research can promise such payoffs. No one can set a deadline for the discovery of the dream mechanism in the brain. The cure for insomnia is not yet in sight. It may be years until we can trace the links between the mind asleep and awake. And who knows what the dream may yet teach us about our own love and hate, hope and fear, ecstasy and rage?

Natural as it is to our species, dreaming remains a confounding human behavior. Our hopes for solving the dream riddle rest on the fact that so much of nature has already been revealed to us through wise and skillful scientific efforts.

We have won some control over viruses we've never seen. We can describe the pit of the earth, where no human has ever traveled. The nucleus of the atom has been split, the distant stars measured, the living cell teased into division, and the human brain responds to the surgeon's touch.

Our scientific efforts have thrown light on the hidden half of the moon. Can we hope to learn the truth about the dark side of the human mind?

Suggestions for Further Reading

Dement, William C. *Some Must Watch While Some Must Sleep.* San Francisco: W. H. Freeman & Co., 1974.

One of the pioneers of modern sleep-dream research gives us a lively personal account of its progress, including ventures, discoveries, dead ends, errors, and achievements.

Faraday, Ann. *The Dream Game.* New York: Harper & Row, Publishers, 1974.

A psychologist offers some intriguing suggestions for recalling and recording, decoding and delving into our own dreams.

Luce, Gay Gaer. *Body Time.* New York: Pantheon Books, Inc., 1971.

The entire subject of biological rhythms, including the REM cycle, is explored in this absorbing book by a skilled science writer.

National Institute of Mental Health. *Current Research on Sleep and Dreams.* Washington, D.C.: U.S. Department of Health, Education, and Welfare, 1973.

This well-written government report includes an excellent summary of the practical results from sleep-dream research, much of which has been sponsored by the National Institute of Mental Health.

Webb, Wilse B. *Sleep: The Gentle Tyrant.* Englewood Cliffs, N.J.: Prentice-Hall, Inc., 1975.

A distinguished scientist in the field of sleep research has written this short book in popular style. It answers many questions about sleep and has a good chapter on dreams.

Woods, Ralph L. and Greenhouse, Herbert B., eds. *The New World of Dreams.* New York: MacMillan Publishing Co., Inc., 1974.

This is a fine collection of writings from ancient times to the present on the subject of dreams.

Index

PRINTED IN U.S.A.